CHICANAS & CHICANOS IN CONTEMPORARY SOCIETY

SECOND EDITION

CHICANAS & CHICANOS IN CONTEMPORARY SOCIETY
Second Edition

Edited by
Roberto M. De Anda

ROWMAN & LITTLEFIELD PUBLISHERS, INC.
Lanham • Boulder • New York • Toronto • Oxford

ROWMAN & LITTLEFIELD PUBLISHERS, INC.

Published in the United States of America
by Rowman & Littlefield Publishers, Inc.
A wholly owned subsidiary of The Rowman & Littlefield Publishing Group, Inc.
4501 Forbes Boulevard, Suite 200, Lanham, Maryland 20706
www.rowmanlittlefield.com

PO Box 317
Oxford
OX2 9RU, UK

British Library Cataloguing in Publication Information Available

Library of Congress Cataloging-in-Publication Data

Chicanas and Chicanos in contemporary society / edited by
  Roberto M. De Anda.—2nd ed.
    p. cm.
  Includes bibliographical references and index.
  ISBN 0-7425-1933-3 (alk. paper) — ISBN 0-7425-1934-1 (pbk. : alk. paper)
  1. Mexican Americans—Social conditions. 2. United States—Ethnic relations.
  3. United States—Social conditions—1980– I. De Anda, Roberto Moreno.
  E184.M5C43 2004
  305.868'72073—dc22   2004002730

Printed in the United States of America

∞™ The paper used in this publication meets the minimum requirements of American
National Standard for Information Sciences—Permanence of Paper for Printed Library
Materials, ANSI/NISO Z39.48-1992.

Contents

Part III: Chicana and Mexicana Mothers' Involvement with Children, Family, and Politics

Part IV: Social Issues in the Chicano/Mexicano Community

Acknowledgments

THIS BOOK OWES ITS EXISTENCE to the contributors, a dedicated group of educators and talented researchers. I am grateful for their trust in me in bringing this collaborative volume to fruition. *¡Mil Gracias!* I would also like to thank Dean Birkenkamp, then editor at Rowman & Littlefield, for his support in the early stages of this book, and his successor, Alan McClare, for seeing to the final product. Many thanks go to Amanda García-Snell for her assistance in preparing the manuscript for publication. Last, but not least, my *compañera,* Hilda Muñoz, deserves a special note of appreciation for her love and faith in me.

Introduction

Roberto M. De Anda

T HIS BOOK DEALS WITH A BROAD RANGE of social issues facing Mexican-origin people in the United States. The studies presented in this volume are brought together by two main themes: (1) social inequalities—cultural, educational, and economic—endured by the Chicano/Mexicano community in the United States and (2) the community's efforts to eradicate the source of those inequalities.

The Mexican-origin population is one of the fastest growing ethnic groups in the United States. In the past decade, the Mexican population grew four times faster than the U.S. population as a whole. Three factors are driving this population growth: the youthfulness of the group, high fertility rates, and immigration. With one-third of people of Mexican descent under the age of fifteen, many of the challenges confronting this community center on the current well-being of children and their future prospects. As a result of increased immigration, today two out of every five people of Mexican descent (Chicanos) were born in Mexico (Saenz, Morales, and Filoteo in chapter 1 of this volume). Regardless of place of birth, however, Chicanos and Mexican immigrants often live in the same communities; their children attend the same schools, they worship in the same churches, and they work side by side. In many ways, their present and future are intertwined.

Several new chapters in the second edition of *Chicanas and Chicanos in Contemporary Society* closely examine issues related to the youthfulness of the Mexican-origin community and its immigrant segment, with particular attention being given to schooling practices and politics. For example, Romero (chapter 3) studies children's ethnic identity formation and its implications for schooling; Moreno (chapter 5) analyzes mother–child interactions and educational outcomes; and Valdez (chapter 6) discusses adolescent motherhood. Other contributions, while not strictly focused on children and youth, discuss issues confronted by young persons. De Anda (chapter 2), for instance, discusses the disadvantaged position of young men in the labor market, and Villa (chapter 8) analyzes poetry by young Chicano prisoners that questions the legitimacy of the criminal justice system.

The significant immigrant presence makes it important to study not only relations between Mexicans and the larger society but also relations within the group—relations between Mexicans born in the United States and those who emigrated from Mexico. Consequently, new chapters take into consideration the immigrant segment of the Mexican-origin community. For instance, Ochoa (chapter 7) documents the struggles of Mexican American and Mexican immigrant mothers to demand better schooling for their children; Valdez (chapter 6) examines generational differences in the experiences of adolescent motherhood; and De Anda (chapter 2) compares labor market outcomes between U.S.-born and Mexican immigrant workers.

To better understand the experiences of this diverse and complex population, the studies offered in this book employ multiple theoretical perspectives and research methods. The studies invoke theories from social science disciplines such as sociology, anthropology, and psychology. Contributors use a variety of research methods, including ethnographic methods and quantitative analysis. Each contributor, however, takes great care to make his or her work accessible to a wide audience without sacrificing theoretical or methodological rigor. The second edition of *Chicanas and Chicanos in Contemporary Society* consists of ten chapters of which seven are new contributions; two have been updated incorporating the most recently available information.

This book is organized into four parts. Part I, "The Mexican-Origin Population and Employment," contains two chapters. Chapter 1, offered by Rogelio Saenz, Maria Cristina Morales, and Janie Filoteo, "The Demography of Mexicans in the United States," examines population change between 1990 and 2000. The authors emphasize that perhaps no other ethnic group in the United States has grown as fast as the Mexican population in the twentieth century. Since the factors driving this population growth—relative young age, fertility, and immigration—are likely to keep exerting their influence, this population is expected to continue to grow in the twenty-first century.

Saenz and his colleagues present a detailed profile of the diverse nature of the Mexican-origin population; they examine the geographic distribution at the national, regional, state, and place level. The authors also describe demographic characteristics such as metropolitan residence, nativity, age/sex distribution, and marriage/family status. The Mexican-origin population has grown more diverse in terms of its geographic distribution as well as its nativity composition.

Chapter 2, presented by Roberto De Anda, is titled "Shortchanged in the Labor Market." His analysis focuses on the causes of underemployment among Mexican workers—joblessness, part-time work, and the working poor. Drawing data from the March 2000 Current Population Survey, he shows that Mexican workers were underemployed twice as often relative to white workers. Further analysis revealed that the highest risk of underemployment was among the very young and poorly educated, recent immigrants, and those employed in blue-collar occupations and periphery industries. De Anda found little evidence that immigrants are responsible for the higher-than-average levels of underemployment among Mexican workers. In order to improve the labor market fortunes of Mexican workers, De Anda argues, greater effort should be placed on offering them a living wage. He also makes a case for workers to organize and fight against discrimination in the labor market.

Part II, "Ethnic Identity Formation and Education: The Experiences of Children and Teachers," includes two chapters. Eric Romero presents chapter 3, "Learning *Manito* Discourse: Children's Stories and Identity in Northern New Mexico." He examines the influence of language socialization and narrative construction on "place identity." Romero argues that place identity is a particularly useful concept to study land-based cultures that incorporate place knowledge into their ethnic identity formation. Romero invokes *querencia* to show that members of a place community share a responsibility to care for the natural environment. His ethnographic study shows that children learn to tell stories that help create and reinforce their *manito* identity, for example, by using Spanish to refer to animals and features of the natural environment. Romero makes a strong call for incorporating children's narratives into schooling practices.

Armando Trujillo, "Teacher Narratives of *Movimiento* Ideology and Bilingual Education" (chapter 4), focuses on the case of Crystal City, Texas, where the Chicano community gained control of social and political institutions through the Raza Unida Party. The political victory of the Raza Unida Party introduced Chicano cultural nationalism, which challenged and replaced the dominant Anglo ideology. Trujillo employs teachers' narratives to gain insights into what *el movimiento* meant for them personally and for their community. In particular, teachers recall that *el movimiento* and the Raza Unida Party instill in them a new sense of cultural pride. Another prominent theme they discuss at length is the relationship between the bilingual/bicultural education program and *movimiento* ideology, and more specifically how they sought to implement the values and ideas of *el movimiento* into educational practices.

Part III, "Chicana and Mexicana Mothers' Involvement with Children, Family, and Politics," consists of three chapters. Robert Moreno, "Exploring Parental Involvement among Mexican American and Latina Mothers" (chapter 5), analyzes factors that predict parental involvement. He also explores the effect of this involvement on their children's educational outcomes. Moreno collected data on 158 mothers who were the primary care providers of their first-grade children. Using quantitative techniques, his findings indicate that while involvement ranged widely, mothers were highly engaged in home-based activities. When examining the predictors of parental involvement, the results support an ecological perspective. Personal, contextual, and sociodemographic factors all play a role in understanding Latina involvement. However, Moreno found limited support for a positive relationship between parental involvement and children's school outcomes. His findings did not show that children of mothers who engaged in more parental involvement activities performed better academically or were better behaved.

In chapter 6, "Chicana Teen Mothers," Elsa Valdez relies on in-depth interviews with adolescent mothers to answer the following questions: What are Chicana adolescent mothers' perceptions of motherhood? Is there a connection between social support networks and self-esteem? Does acculturation affect social support systems? Valdez found that social networks—the extended family but most importantly mothers—provide instrumental support (e.g., clothing and diapers) and emotional support. The respondents' social networks also enhanced their self-esteem. Her data also revealed that despite acculturation, the importance of close family ties remained high. Although one in five of the respondents considered motherhood a burden, the majority perceived motherhood in positive terms. Finally, Valdez makes a strong call for the creation of a research and policy center on Latino children and adolescents' issues.

The study by Gilda Ochoa, chapter 7, "Let's Unite So That Our Children Are Better Off Than Us," examines political cooperation between Mexican American and Mexican immigrant women to challenge an English-only initiative in a school district in the Los Angeles area. Ochoa analyzes the activities of a group of working-class women who founded Parents for Quality Education, a group that supports bilingual education in the Los Angeles area. Their efforts were successful until the passage of Proposition 227, which effectively ended bilingual education in California. Ochoa focuses on the activists' strategies and practices that led to generating support for bilingual education.

Part IV, "Social Issues in the Chicano/Mexicano Community," has three chapters. Raúl Villa, "Of *Corridos* and Convicts" (chapter 8), examines the experiences of *pintos* (Chicano convicts) through their poetry. The unfair treatment of Mexican-origin people in the criminal justice system has been documented in *corridos,* or ballads. Villa's study links the traditional *corrido* to contemporary *pinto* poetry. In both types of narratives, the protagonists, who are seen as the criminal, are exonerated and the Anglo criminal justice system is revealed as the real culprit. His study shows a continuum of how basic ideas have been used and improved by recent *pinto* poets to challenge the dominant power structure rather than passively accept violated rights.

In "*Festejando* Community" (chapter 9), Elizabeth Flores documents the origins and development of Fiesta Mexicana, a celebration of community in Woodburn, Oregon, a small city with deep agricultural roots. Woodburn is located in the fertile Willamette Valley about thirty miles south of Portland. Flores traces changes in the tastes and sounds of fiesta over the years. Until the early 1950s, when Mexican American farmworkers from Texas began to settle out of the migrant stream, Woodburn was a predominantly Anglo community. In the past few years, however, Woodburn has experienced an influx of immigrants from Mexico. Fiesta was established to celebrate the presence of this group. Changes in the food, music, and events at fiesta parallel changes in the composition of the residents of Mexican descent in the community.

Gilbert Cadena and Lara Medina close the compilation with chapter 10, "Liberation Theology and Social Change." The authors argue that a Chicana/Chicano-based theology of liberation emphasizing social action is gaining momentum in challenging the Catholic Church. While the church has historically prevailed over the spiritual life of Chicano/Mexicano community, there is growing discontent among the laity. They view the church as a rigid hierarchy that is unwilling to bring about needed change. Just as the number of worshipers of Mexican descent is growing, others are leaving the church. Social scientists predict that in the not too distant future Latinos will be about half of the Catholic laity: The Catholic Church is poised to become a Latino Church. Cadena and Medina point out that Chicanos are challenging the church at the same time that the church is being challenged from within. Cadena and Medina present a persuasive argument about the challenges to the church from liberation theology and *mujerista* theologians; the latter focus on the interplay of social, class, and gender oppression that affects Latinas. The authors discuss concrete examples of challenges to the church coming from liberation theology, *mujerista* theology, and *calpulli*—a cooperative system based on indigenous cultural practices organized in base communities struggling for social change.

PART I

THE MEXICAN-ORIGIN POPULATION AND EMPLOYMENT

1

The Demography of Mexicans in the United States

Rogelio Saenz, Maria Cristina Morales, and Janie Filoteo

THE MEXICAN-ORIGIN POPULATION is one of the most dynamic ethnic groups in the United States.[1] During the twentieth century it grew more rapidly than any other group. While the country's total population tripled from 92 million in 1910 to 281.4 million in 2000, the Mexican population expanded from 367,500 to 20.6 million in the same time span. Over the past decade, the Mexican population increased four times faster (52.9 percent) than the overall U.S. total population (13.2 percent). Few other ethnic groups in the nation can match this contemporary growth pattern. Today, Mexicans—the largest segment of the Latino population—represent the second largest specific minority group in the nation, trailing only African Americans.

Mexican population growth has been caused by three factors: (1) Mexicans tend to be relatively young compared to other groups in the nation, (2) Mexicans traditionally have higher fertility rates, and (3) the Mexican population has been supplemented by large flows of immigrants, both legal and illegal, especially since the 1960s. Population estimates by the U.S. Census Bureau (2000a,b) suggest that immigrants accounted for nearly two-thirds (65.2 percent) of the growth of the overall Latino population between 1990 and 1999. These three demographic factors supply the potential for further growth in the Mexican population over the coming decades.

Historically, the Mexican population has been disproportionately located in the Southwest region. Approximately three-fourths of the country's Mexicans were found in the Southwest in 2000, down from more than four-fifths in 1990. Clearly a significant shift away from the Southwest took place in the

1990s. Unfortunately, much of our knowledge of the Mexican population has been based almost solely on the Southwest.

This chapter seeks to provide an in-depth overview of the demographic attributes of the Mexican population in the United States overall and in five regions of the country. Before undertaking the analysis, however, we will establish a historical demographic perspective.

Historical Demographic Context

The Mexican-origin ethnic group has a long history in this country. Its ancestors explored and established settlements in parts of the Southwest long before European immigrants landed in Plymouth Rock (Saenz 1999). The incorporation of Mexicans into the United States came about through conflict between the United States and Mexico—first with the annexation of Texas in 1845 after the independence of Texas from Mexico, and later with the signing of the Treaty of Guadalupe Hidalgo in 1848 at the conclusion of the Mexican-American War. The Mexican-origin population has grown significantly since the initial cohort of Mexicans who became U.S. citizens during this period. Unfortunately, there is a dearth of historical demographic statistics enumerating the Mexican-origin population, with specific data for Mexicans completely lacking or plagued by inconsistent definitions. For example, the definition of persons of Mexican origin has varied over time from Mexicans being treated as a racial category, to the presence of a Spanish surname, to the use of the Spanish language. Fortunately, since the 1980 census, people have been allowed to identify themselves as Hispanic-origin and the specific Hispanic subgroup to which they belong.

While historical information on the population size of Mexicans in the United States is lacking, much of the growth has been due to immigration. According to the U.S. Immigration and Naturalization Service (2000), slightly more than 5.8 million Mexicans immigrated to the United States legally between 1820 and 1998 (table 1.1), making Mexico the second largest sender of immigrants during the period behind Germany (nearly 7.2 million immigrants). This figure, however, does not include the large number of Mexicans who arrived as undocumented immigrants. Yet Mexican immigration to the United States is a twentieth-century phenomenon. Of the slightly more than 5.8 million Mexicans who immigrated to the United States legally from 1820 to 1998, only 0.5 percent (or about 28,000) immigrated between 1820 and 1900. The first major wave of Mexican immigration to the United States occurred in the 1910s and 1920s when many Mexicans fled the Mexican Revolution. Mexican immigrants coming legally at this time accounted for approximately one-eighth (11.7 percent or about 678,000) of all legal Mexican immigrants between 1820 and 1998. The flow of immigrants coming to this country during the period, however, continued to be dominated by Europeans.

TABLE 1.1
Number of Mexican Legal Immigrants
Entering the United States, 1820–1998

Period	Number Mexican Immigrants	% of Total Mexican Immigrants Over 1820–1998	Cum. % Immigrants 1820–1998
1820	1	0.00	0.00
1821–1830	4,817	0.08	0.08
1831–1840	6,599	0.11	0.20
1841–1850	3,271	0.06	0.25
1851–1860	3,078	0.05	0.31
1861–1870	2,191	0.04	0.34
1871–1880	5,162	0.09	0.43
1881–1890	1,913	0.03	0.46
1891–1900	971	0.02	0.48
1901–1910	49,642	0.85	1.33
1911–1920	219,004	3.76	5.10
1921–1930	459,287	7.89	12.99
1931–1940	22,319	0.38	13.37
1941–1950	60,589	1.04	14.41
1951–1960	299,811	5.15	19.56
1961–1970	453,937	7.80	27.36
1971–1980	640,294	11.00	38.37
1981–1990	1,655,843	28.45	66.82
1991–1998	1,931,237	33.18	100.00
Total	5,819,966	100.00	100.00

Source: U.S. Immigration and Naturalization Service, 2000.
Note: The data are based on country of last residence rather than country of birth.

The ethnic composition of U.S. immigration has changed dramatically since the 1960s. From 1961 to 1998, Mexico has been the major sender of immigrants to the United States, with nearly 4.7 million Mexicans (or 80 percent of all Mexicans who have entered legally between 1820 and 1998) immigrating legally to the United States during the period. The heavy immigrant flow was due in part to the Immigration Act of 1965 and its emphasis on family reunification. Furthermore, the Immigration Reform and Control Act (IRCA) of 1986 allowed many Mexican undocumented immigrants to legalize their status (Bean, Edmonston, and Passel 1990; U.S. Immigration and Naturalization Service 1992). Mexicans accounted for approximately three-fourths of the three million persons who gained legal status through IRCA (Chavez 1996). Between 1991 and 1998, slightly more than 1.9 million Mexican immigrants entered the country legally, accounting for one-third of all Mexican legal immigrants between 1820 and 1998. Moreover, the March 2000 Current Population Survey (U.S. Census Bureau 2001a) indicated that Mexicans made up 28 percent of the foreign-born population living in the United States in 2000, the highest level since the 30 percent mark of Germans in 1830.

This historical demographic perspective illustrates the unique position of the Mexican-origin population. This population is one that has a long, well-established presence in this country, but it also accounts for the majority of recent immigrants (Saenz 1999). This combination of newcomers and old-timers is largely responsible for the diverse nature of the Mexican population. The Mexican-origin population includes people who trace their roots in this country back to the late 1840s as well as those who have recently crossed the border into the United States.

Analysis Plan and Data Sources

The following analyses provide a general overview of the demography of the Mexican population in the United States. First, we examine the population and geographic distribution patterns among Mexicans for the 1990–2000 period. Data for this part of the analysis come from the 1990 and 2000 censuses and are obtained directly from the Inter-University Program for Latino Research (2001, 2002). The analysis is conducted at the national, regional, state, and place levels. Second, we use data from the American Community Supplementary Survey 2000 Public Use Microdata Sample (PUMS) (U.S. Census Bureau 2002) and from the March 2000 Current Population Survey (CPS) (U.S. Census Bureau 2001a,b) to develop a profile for Mexicans with respect to demographic attributes (e.g., metropolitan residence, nativity, age/sex distribution, and marriage/family characteristics).

The data for the Mexican-origin population are based on individuals who defined themselves as "Hispanic/Latino" and more specifically as "Mexican." For comparative purposes, we present data for the U.S. total population to assess the similarities and differences between the demographic patterns of Mexicans and the overall national population.

The analysis will present data for the Mexican population at the national and regional levels. Although the U.S. Census Bureau categorizes the U.S. states and the District of Columbia into four regions (Midwest, South, West, and Northeast), we make some alterations to develop an additional region, the Southwest, to account for the concentration of Mexicans in the five states (Arizona, California, Colorado, New Mexico, and Texas) that compose this region. The reader should keep in mind that the West region as used here does not include Arizona, California, Colorado, and New Mexico, while the South region does not contain Texas.[2]

The Demography of the Mexican-Origin Population

In this section, we provide an overview of the population and geographic distribution patterns of Mexicans as well as a demographic profile of Mexicans in the country and in the five regions. We begin the analysis with an analysis of the population and geographic distribution patterns of the Mexican population.

Population and Geographic Distribution Patterns

According to the 2000 Census, there were approximately 20.6 million Mexicans in the United States in 2000 (table 1.2). Thus, in absolute numbers the

TABLE 1.2
**Population Characteristics for Mexican and
U.S. Population by Region, 1980–2000**

Region	Mexican		U.S. Total	
	1990	*2000*	*1990*	*2000*
Population Size				
Southwest	11,237,325	15,374,276	55,221,222	65,974,407
Midwest	1,153,296	2,200,196	59,668,632	64,392,776
West	477,618	1,110,952	14,551,370	18,075,345
South	452,703	1,476,118	68,459,420	79,385,000
Northeast	174,996	479,169	50,809,229	53,594,378
Total	13,495,938	20,640,711	248,709,873	281,421,906
% Distribution				
Southwest	83.3	74.5	22.2	23.4
Midwest	8.5	10.7	24.0	22.9
West	3.5	5.4	5.9	6.4
South	3.4	7.2	27.5	28.2
Northeast	1.3	2.3	20.4	19.0
Total	100.0	100.0	100.0	100.0
% Region's Population				
Southwest	20.3	23.3	—	—
Midwest	1.9	3.4	—	—
West	3.3	6.1	—	—
South	0.7	1.9	—	—
Northeast	0.3	0.9	—	—

Source: Inter-University Program for Latino Research (2001).

Mexican population increased by 7.1 million between 1990 and 2000, with about 58 percent (or 4.1 million) of this growth centered in the Southwest region. During the same period, the entire U.S. population increased almost 32.7 million. This suggests that although Mexicans accounted for only 7.3 percent of the nation's population in 2000, they accounted for 21.8 percent of the 32.7 million inhabitants added to the U.S. population through natural increase and immigration between 1990 and 2000.

The growth in the Mexican population during the 1990s can be further illustrated by examining the relative growth during the decade (figure 1.1). Overall, the Mexican population increased at a rate (52.9 percent) that was four times faster than that of the U.S. total population (13.2 percent) between 1990 and 2000. The rapid growth of the Mexican population relative to the total population is also apparent across the different regions. The Mexican population grew the most rapidly in the South (226.1 percent), where the number of Mexicans more than tripled, the Northeast (173.8), the West (132.6 percent), and the Midwest (90.8 percent) during the decade. In contrast, the Mexican population grew the most slowly in the Southwest (36.8 percent), although the growth was much more rapid than the region's overall population growth (19.5 percent).

The Mexican population continues to be predominately located in the Southwest region, with 74.5 percent of all Mexicans making their home in the region in 2000 (table 1.2). Close to 11 percent live in the Midwest, slightly more than 7 percent live in the South, and more than 5 percent live in the West. Relatively few (2.3 percent) Mexicans live in the Northeast. Proportionately speaking, Mexicans are over three times more likely to be located in the Southwest compared to the total population. However, it is clear that the geographic distribution of the Mexican population shifted significantly during the 1990s. Indeed, the Southwest region's share of the Mexican population in the nation dropped from 83.3 percent in 1990 to 74.5 percent in 2000, while the share of each of the other regions rose. Remarkably, in the South the regional share of Mexicans doubled from 3.4 percent in 1990 to 7.2 percent in 2000.

Nonetheless, the Mexican-origin population composes a significant portion (23.3 percent) of the total population of the Southwest (see table 1.2). The Mexican population makes up a relatively small share of the populations of the other four regions, with Mexicans having the highest proportional representation (about one of every 16 residents) in the West and the lowest (about one of every 100 residents) in the Northeast.

Population Patterns at the State Level

The number of Mexicans at the state level varies greatly from a low of 1,174 in Vermont to nearly 8.5 million in California (table 1.3). The top ten most

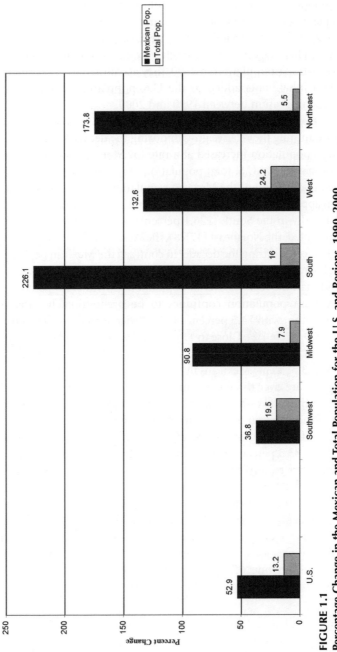

FIGURE 1.1
Percentage Change in the Mexican and Total Population for the U.S. and Regions, 1990–2000

populous states with respect to Mexicans include California (8,455,926), Texas (5,071,963), Illinois (1,144,390), Arizona (1,065,578), Colorado (450,760), Florida (363,925), New Mexico (330,049), Washington (329,934), Nevada (285,764), and Georgia (275,288). Together, these ten states contain 86 percent (or nearly 17.8 million) of the nation's Mexican-origin population. However, California and Texas together contained nearly two-thirds (65.5 percent) of Mexicans in the nation.

In a relative sense, Mexicans accounted for one-fourth of the populations of California and Texas and one-fifth of the inhabitants of Arizona. They made up at least one-tenth of the populations of three other states: New Mexico (18.1 percent), Nevada (14.3 percent), and Colorado (10.5 percent). In sixteen states located in the Northeast, South, and Midwest, Mexicans accounted for less than 1 percent of the population.

TABLE 1.3
Total and Mexican Population by State, 2000

State	Total Pop.	Mexican Pop.	State	Total Pop.	Mexican Pop.
Alabama	4,447,100	44,522	Montana	902,195	11,735
Alaska	626,932	13,334	Nebraska	1,711,263	71,030
Arizona	5,130,632	1,065,578	Nevada	1,998,257	285,764
Arkansas	2,673,400	61,204	New Hampshire	1,235,786	4,590
California	33,871,648	8,455,926	New Jersey	8,414,350	102,929
Colorado	4,301,261	450,760	New Mexico	1,819,046	330,049
Connecticut	3,405,565	23,484	New York	18,976,457	260,889
Delaware	783,600	12,986	North Carolina	8,049,313	246,545
Dist. of Col.	572,059	5,098	North Dakota	642,200	4,295
Florida	15,982,378	363,925	Ohio	11,353,140	90,663
Georgia	8,186,453	275,288	Oklahoma	3,450,654	132,813
Hawaii	1,211,537	19,820	Oregon	3,421,399	214,662
Idaho	1,293,953	79,324	Pennsylvania	12,281,054	55,178
Illinois	12,419,293	1,144,390	Rhode Island	1,048,319	5,881
Indiana	6,080,485	153,042	South Carolina	4,012,012	52,871
Iowa	2,926,324	61,154	South Dakota	754,844	6,364
Kansas	2,688,418	148,270	Tennessee	5,689,283	77,372
Kentucky	4,041,769	31,385	Texas	20,851,820	5,071,963
Louisiana	4,468,976	32,267	Utah	2,233,169	136,416
Maine	1,274,923	2,756	Vermont	608,827	1,174
Maryland	5,296,486	39,900	Virginia	7,078,515	73,979
Massachusetts	6,349,097	22,288	Washington	5,894,121	329,934
Michigan	9,938,444	220,769	West Virginia	1,808,344	4,347
Minnesota	4,919,479	95,613	Wisconsin	5,363,675	126,719
Mississippi	2,844,658	21,616	Wyoming	493,782	19,963
Missouri	5,595,211	77,887			

Source: Inter-University Program for Latino Research (2001).

States varied greatly, however, in the absolute and relative growth in the Mexican-origin population between 1990 and 2000. In absolute terms, California and Texas together accounted for one of every two of the additional 7.1 million Mexicans added to the national population between 1990 and 2000. However, states outside of the Southwest tended to grow more rapidly in a relative sense. Twenty-eight states saw their Mexican populations more than double between 1990 and 2000, none located in the Southwest. In North Carolina the Mexican population increased more than sevenfold from 32,670 in 1990 to 246,545 in 2000, and Georgia it increased by a factor of 5.5 from 49,182 in 1990 to 275,288 in 2000. Five other states saw their Mexican populations more than quadruple during the period: Tennessee (457.5 percent increase from 13,879 to 77,372), Arkansas (389.8 percent increase from 12,496 to 61,204), South Carolina (379.4 percent increase from 11,028 to 52,871), Alabama (368.2 percent increase from 9,509 to 44,522), and Delaware (321.2 percent increase from 3,083 to 12,986). Much of this growth in the South and Midwest was due to their recruitment into beef, pork, and poultry processing jobs (Gouveia and Saenz 2000; Stull, Broadway, and Griffith 1995).

Population Patterns at the Place Level

The large presence of Mexicans in the Southwest, however, can also be illustrated at the place level. The left-hand part of table 1.4 contains a list of the twenty places with the largest Mexican-origin populations in 2000, with all but two (Chicago and New York) located in the Southwest and fifteen of the twenty located in California and Texas. The ten places with the largest number of Mexicans include Los Angeles, CA (1,091,686), Chicago, IL (530,462), Houston, TX (527,442), San Antonio, TX (473,420), Phoenix, AZ (375,096), El Paso, TX (359,699), Dallas, TX (350,491), San Diego, CA (259,219), Santa Ana, CA (222,719), and San Jose, CA (221,148). It should be noted that the populations of these places are for the city itself and do not include the population of surrounding communities that compose the metropolitan statistical area (MSA). Thus, the populations of the MSAs would be larger than those of the individual places.

There are numerous places, especially in the Southwest, where Mexicans represent the numerical majority population. Mexicans make up at least half of the populations of 308 of the 1,661 cities, census designated places (CDPs), towns, and villages across the United States that contained at least one person of Mexican origin in 2000. Of these 308 geographic places, the greatest number are in Texas (129) and California (127), with the remainder located in Arizona (20), Washington (13), New Mexico (8), Florida (5), Illinois (2), Colorado (1), Georgia (1), Nevada (1), and Oregon (1).

TABLE 1.4
Top Twenty Places in the United States with the Largest
Absolute and Relative Mexican Populations, 2000

Rank	City	Mexican Population	City	% Mexican
1	Los Angeles, CA	1,091,686	Progresso, TX	93.6
2	Chicago, IL	530,462	Presidio, TX	89.9
3	Houston, TX	527,442	Alton, TX	89.6
4	San Antonio, TX	473,420	Hidalgo, TX	89.4 (4)
5	Phoenix, AZ	375,096	Cactus, TX	89.4 (4)
6	El Paso, TX	359,699	Penitas, TX	89.4 (4)
7	Dallas, TX	350,491	Palmview, TX	89.2
8	San Diego, CA	259,219	Roma, TX	88.8
9	Santa Ana, CA	222,719	Calexico, CA	87.7
10	San Jose, CA	221,148	Somerton, AZ	87.4
11	New York, NY	186,872	Coachella, CA	87.2
12	Austin, TX	153,868	Huron, CA	86.9
13	Tucson, AZ	145,234	Parlier, CA	86.4
14	Fresno, CA	144,772	San Juan, TX	84.5
15	Laredo, TX	133,185	La Joya, TX	83.9
16	Fort Worth, TX	132,894	East Los Angeles, CA	83.9
17	Long Beach, CA	127,129	San Joaquin, CA	83.2
18	Anaheim, CA	126,017	San Luis, AZ	83.0
19	Denver, CO	120,664	Sunland Park, NM	82.7 (19)
20	East Los Angeles, CA	104,223	Palmhurst, TX	82.7 (19)

Source: Inter-University Program for Latino Research (2002).

The right-hand part of table 1.4 contains the top twenty places having the highest levels of Mexican proportional representation. Note that the list excludes CDPs, towns, and villages due to their relatively small population sizes, with the one exception being East Los Angeles (a large CDP), which is included in the list. Mexicans compose at least 82.7 percent of the populations of these places, located in Texas (11), California (6), Arizona (2), and New Mexico (1). However, the top-twenty list is dominated by places located in the Lower Rio Grande Valley of Texas, the southernmost part of Texas, with eight of the twenty located in this region. The top ten places where Mexicans account for the highest proportion of the population include Progresso, TX (93.6 percent), Presidio, TX (89.9 percent), Alton, TX (89.6 percent), Hidalgo, TX (89.4 percent), Cactus, TX (89.4 percent), Penitas, TX (89.4 percent), Palmview, TX (89.2 percent), Roma, TX (88.8 percent), Calexico, CA (87.7 percent), and Somerton, AZ (87.4 percent).

Demographic Characteristics of Mexicans Across Regions

This section analyzes the demographic characteristics of the Mexican population with respect to metropolitan residence, nativity, age/sex distribution, and marriage/family characteristics. This part of the analysis is based on data from the American Community Supplementary Survey 2000 Public Use Microdata Sample (PUMS) and the March 2000 Current Population Survey (CPS). It introduces data for Mexicans living in the United States overall and the five regions, as well as reference data for the U.S. total population.

Metropolitan Residence

The Mexican population tends to be overwhelmingly located in metropolitan areas. Overall, approximately 90 percent of Mexicans make their homes in metropolitan areas, compared to about 81 percent of the nation's entire population (table 1.5). Mexicans tend to be concentrated in the central cities

TABLE 1.5
General Demographic Characteristics of Mexicans by Region, 2000

Selected Characteristics	Total	Southwest	Midwest	West	South	Northeast
Metro residence:						
% in Metro areas	89.8	91.2	86.5	74.1	85.2	98.2
Nativity:						
% Foreign-born	40.7	38.2	44.1	41.3	57.7	57.4
Age/sex:						
% Less than 15	31.9	32.2	32.2	32.9	28.7	30.1
% 65 and older	4.0	4.5	2.8	2.2	2.1	2.4
Sex ratio	109.8	105.5	125.0	113.4	132.1	126.5
Marriage/family:						
% Fam. HHs with Fem. householder, No husband present	20.0	21.5	12.6	15.6	15.9	18.6
% 25–44 Age-group Currently married:						
Males	65.2	65.6	64.0	68.4	57.7	74.0
Females	66.7	65.8	71.2	73.2	66.4	68.7
% Females 15–49 Having baby within the last year	10.0	9.7	10.6	7.2	14.7	10.6

Sources: The metro residence data are obtained from the 2000 Current Population Survey March 2000 Supplement (U.S. Census Bureau 2001) and the remaining data are obtained from the American Community Survey Supplementary Survey 2000 Public Use Microdata Sample (PUMS) (U.S. Census Bureau 2002).
Note: The metro residence data are based on persons sixteen years of age and older.

while the total population is more likely to reside in suburbs. Across the regions, Mexicans have the highest degree of metropolitan residence in the Northeast (98.2 percent) and Southwest (91.2 percent). In contrast, slightly over one-fourth of Mexicans in the West and roughly one-seventh of those in the South and Midwest are located in nonmetropolitan areas.

Nativity

As noted earlier, immigrants represent a major portion of the Mexican-origin population. Overall, foreign-born persons make up two-fifths (40.7 percent) of the Mexican population in the country (table 1.5), compared to only one-ninth (11.1 percent) of the overall U.S. population. Foreign-born persons are the most represented in the South (57.7 percent) and Northeast (57.4 percent), where they compose nearly three-fifths of the Mexican populations of each of these regions. By way of contrast, less than two-fifths (38.2 percent) of Mexicans in the Southwest are foreign-born.

Age/Sex Distribution

Given the unique demographic patterns of Mexicans, the age/sex structure of the Mexican population differs noticeably from that of the national population. The Mexican population is quite young. About one of every three (31.9 percent) Mexicans in the United States was under fifteen years of age in 2000 (table 1.5). In contrast, this age-group made up only slightly more than one of every five (21.9 percent) in the overall U.S. population. On the other hand, elderly persons sixty-five years and older accounted for only one of every twenty-five (4 percent) persons in the Mexican population, while seniors constituted about one of every eight (12.1 percent) in the overall U.S. population. Within the Mexican population, persons less than fifteen years of age accounted for approximately one-third of the populations of the West (32.9 percent), Southwest (32.2 percent), and Midwest (32.2 percent), while the elderly were most well represented in the Southwest (4.5 percent).

The age composition of the Mexican-origin population can be illustrated graphically with an age/sex pyramid, a bar graph containing bars for successive age-groups from the youngest at the base to the oldest at the top, with males represented on the left side of the graph and females on the right side. The width of each bar denotes the size of a given age/sex group relative to the total population according to the percentage scale on the horizontal axis.

The age/sex pyramid for the Mexican population in the nation and the U.S. total population in 2000 appear in figures 1.2a and 1.2b. The shape of the two pyramids differs significantly, reflecting major differences in the age/sex structure of the two populations. The youthfulness of the Mexican population is evident by the wide bars at the base. For example, males and females less than five years of age together account for 11 percent of the entire Mexican population (compared to 7 percent in the case of the U.S. total population). The immigration influence is evident in the wide bars associated with the 20–24 and 25–29 age-groups for Mexicans. Males in these age-groups represent a significantly larger proportion of the entire population (11.2 percent) than do their female counterparts (9.2 percent), with the respective percentages being smaller even among the U.S. total population (males, 6.5 percent; females, 6.6 percent). The pointed top of the Mexican pyramid reflects the relative scarcity of the elderly in this population, while the comparatively wider top in the U.S. total population shows the older structure of the overall national population.

Sex distribution data reveal that males outnumber females within the Mexican population. Demographers use the sex ratio (number of males per 100 females) to assess the sex distribution of given populations. The overall sex ratio for the Mexican population is 109.8, a figure that is quite different from that of the U.S. total population (95.4), where females outnumber males (table 1.5). This discrepancy is due to the young age structure and large prevalence of immigrants among the Mexican population. Males outnumber females within the Mexican population to the greatest extent in three regions that have sex ratios of at least 125: South (132.1), Northeast (126.5), and Midwest (125.0).

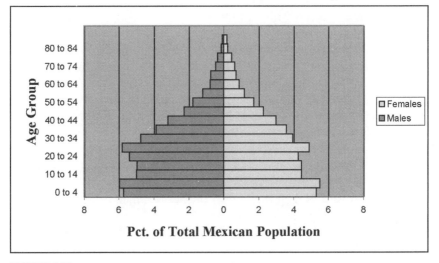

FIGURE 1.2A
Age-Sex Pyramid for the Mexican Population, 2000

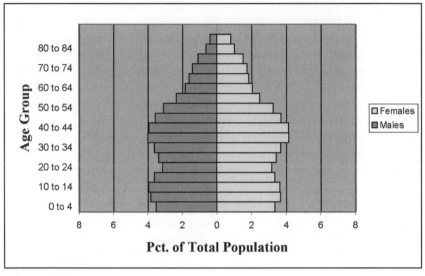

FIGURE 1.2B
Age-Sex Pyramid for the Total U.S. Population, 2000

Marriage/Family Characteristics

The marriage and family characteristics of Mexicans also tend to differ from those of the general population. Overall, one-fifth of Mexican families had female householders without a husband present (table 1.5), whereas such families formed a somewhat lower percentage (18.4 percent) of families among the U.S. total population. This type of family is the most prevalent among Mexicans in the Southwest (21.5 percent) and the least prevalent in the Midwest (12.6 percent).

We also use data to assess the prevalence of marriage among Mexicans 25–44 years of age. Two-thirds of Mexican men and women in this age-group are currently married, compared to about three-fifths of their peers in the U.S. total population (table 1.5). The subgroups within the Mexican population that are the most likely to be currently married include men in the Northeast (74.0 percent) and women in the West (73.2 percent) and Midwest (71.2 percent). In contrast, less than three-fifths of Mexican men in the South (57.7 percent) are currently married.

Other data indicate the extent to which Mexican women of childbearing age (15–49) gave birth within one year of the 2000 census. Overall, one-tenth of Mexican women in the 15–44 age category had a baby in the previous year, compared to a lower percentage (5.9 percent) among women in the overall national population (table 1.5). Within the Mexican population, the level of fertility within the last year ranged from a low of 7.2 percent among Mexican women in the South to a high of 14.7 percent among those in the West.

Conclusion

This chapter has presented an overview of the demography of the Mexican-origin population in the United States. The Mexican population has grown tremendously during the twentieth century and continues to grow at a rapid rate, outpacing the growth of most other ethnic groups in the country. While Mexicans accounted for only 7.3 percent of the nation's population, they were responsible for nearly 22 percent of the 32.7 million people added to the overall U.S. population through natural increase and immigration between 1990 and 2000.

The large-scale growth of the Mexican population is likely to continue through the twenty-first century due to the group's young age structure, high fertility rates, and continued immigration from Mexico. Under this realistic scenario, the Mexican population is likely to continue to account for major portions of the future growth of the national population. In addition, the group's relative share of the U.S. population is likely to rise as well. People in both the public and private sectors will have to pay increasing attention to the Mexican population because of its tremendous growth and related impact on different societal institutions. We call on policymakers in particular to devote more attention to the plight of Mexicans in such areas as education, training, and employment. The combination of a young age structure along with a low level of education requires immediate attention to address the problems that members of this group encounter. Failure to deal with the problems of this population today could potentially result in massive social and economic problems in the future, with Mexicans ill prepared to compete effectively in an increasingly technological workforce.

Undoubtedly the most important trend arising in the 1990s has been the shifting geographic distribution of the Mexican population. While it is still true that Mexicans continue to be clustered in the Southwest, this region experienced a drop in its share of the national Mexican population from 83.3 percent in 1990 to 74.5 percent in 2000. All other regions increased their share of the Mexican population. The Mexican population is increasingly fanning out to points beyond the Southwest. Between 1990 and 2000, the Mexican population more than tripled in the South, nearly tripled in the Northeast, more than doubled in the West, and nearly doubled in the Midwest. This suggests that other regions of the country, aside from the Southwest, are likely to experience varying patterns of population change associated with the growth of the Mexican-origin population. Mexicans in the five regions vary to a certain extent on the different characteristics examined here. Clearly immigration continues to be a prominent feature in the experience of Mexicans in the United States. Thus, the Mexican-origin population is quite diverse. This chapter has provided a demographic knowledge intended to enhance the reader's understanding of the more substantive aspects of the Mexican-origin population presented in the remainder of the book.

Notes

1. In this chapter the terms "Mexican" and "Mexican-origin" are used interchangeably to refer to the population under study. These terms do not take into account nativity status and are meant to capture the diverse nature of the Mexican-origin population.

2. The Southwest includes Arizona, California, Colorado, New Mexico, and Texas. The Midwest comprises Illinois, Indiana, Iowa, Kansas, Michigan, Minnesota, Missouri, Nebraska, North Dakota, Ohio, South Dakota, and Wisconsin. The West is made up of Alaska, Hawaii, Idaho, Montana, Nevada, Oregon, Utah, Washington, and Wyoming. The South is composed of Alabama, Arkansas, Delaware, the District of Columbia, Florida, Georgia, Kentucky, Louisiana, Maryland, Mississippi, North Carolina, Oklahoma, South Carolina, Tennessee, Virginia, and West Virginia. The Northeast includes Connecticut, Maine, Massachusetts, New Hampshire, New Jersey, New York, Pennsylvania, Rhode Island, and Vermont.

References

Bean, Frank D., Barry Edmonston, and Jeffrey S. Passel, eds. 1990. *Undocumented Migration to the United States: IRCA and the Experience of the 1980s.* Washington, DC: Urban Institute Press.

Chavez, Leo R. 1996. "Borders and Bridges: Undocumented Immigrants from Mexico and Central America." In *Origins and Destinations: Immigration, Race, and Ethnicity in America,* ed. Silvia Pedraza and Ruben G. Rumbaut, 250–62. Belmont, CA: Wadsworth.

Gouveia, Lourdes, and Rogelio Saenz. 2000. "Global Forces and Latino Population Growth in the Midwest: A Regional and Subregional Analysis." *Great Plains Research* 10: 305–28.

Inter-University Program for Latino Research. *Population Change for Mexican by State.* 2001. Notre Dame, IN: Inter-University Program for Latino Research, Census Information Center, 2001. www.nd.edu/ percent7Eiuplr/cic/origin_data.html (September 7, 2001).

———. *Population Change for Mexican by Place*. 2002. Notre Dame, IN: Inter-University Program for Latino Research, Census Information Center. www.nd.edu/percent7Eiuplr/cic/ethnic_place_htmlfiles/ethnic_place_data.html (revised January 20, 2002).

Saenz, Rogelio. 1999. "Mexican Americans." In *The Minority Report: An Introduction to Racial, Ethnic, and Gender Relations*, ed. A. Gary Dworkin and Rosalind J. Dworkin, 209–29. Fort Worth, TX: Holt, Rinehart & Winston.

Stull, Donald D., Michael J. Broadway, and David Griffith, eds. 1995. *Any Way You Cut It: Meat Processing and Small Town America*. Lawrence, KS: University Press of Kansas.

U.S. Census Bureau. 2002. *American Community Survey Supplementary Survey 2000 Public Use Microdata Sample (PUMS)*. Washington, DC: U.S. Census Bureau. www.census.gov/acs/www/Products/PUMS (revised August 22, 2002).

———. 2001a. *Current Population Survey March 2000 Supplement*. Washington, DC: U.S. Census Bureau and the Bureau for Labor Statistics, 2001. www.bls.census.gov/cps/ads/2000/sdata.htm (July 6, 2001).

———. 2001b. *Profile of the Foreign-Born Population in the United States*. Current Population Reports, P23-206. Washington, DC: U.S. Bureau of the Census.

———. 2000a. *Foreign-Born Resident Population Estimates of the United States by Sex, Race, and Hispanic Origin: April 1, 1999 to July 1, 1999*. Washington, DC: U.S. Census Bureau. http://eire.census.gov/popest/archives/national/us_nativity/fbtab003.txt (April 11, 2000).

———. 2000b. *Native Resident Population Estimates of the United States by Sex, Race, and Hispanic Origin: April 1, 1999 to July 1, 1999*. Washington, DC: U.S. Census Bureau, 2000b. http://eire.census.gov/popest/archives/national/us_nativity/nbtab003.txt (April 11, 2000).

U. S. Immigration and Naturalization Service. 2000. *1998 Statistical Yearbook of the Immigration and Naturalization Service*. Washington, DC: U. S. Department of Justice.

———. 1992. *Immigration Statistics: Fiscal Year 1991 (Advanced Report)*. Washington, DC: U.S. Department of Justice.

2

Shortchanged in the Labor Market: Underemployed Mexican-Origin Men

Roberto M. De Anda

ALTHOUGH MANY MEXICAN-ORIGIN WORKERS have made gains in the labor market by getting better jobs and better wages during the last few decades, others are being left behind. Those who are not moving up usually lack steady work; they go from one job to another or work part-time. Others, despite working full-time, do not earn enough to make ends meet. The following short stories illustrate the experiences of these workers in the labor market.

Henry is a young man in his late twenties. He is married and has a daughter. After dropping out of high school, Henry held a string of low-paying dead-end jobs, for example, parking lot attendant, janitor, and groundskeeper. When he is not working, he depends on meager unemployment insurance benefits. He and his wife rent an apartment in a neighborhood with a high crime rate. They would like to save money to buy a home in a safer area but have been unable to do so. Henry's employers typically do not supply medical insurance. Fortunately, he and his wife are very healthy, but when their daughter gets sick they have to borrow money to get her medical care.

José, a high school graduate, works as a welder in a small company that makes electronic equipment for airplanes. When José works full-time, he earns good money and gets excellent fringe benefits. But when the demand for airplanes is low, his boss gets fewer work orders and cuts back the number of hours that José works per week. On average, José has been working about twenty hours per week and his benefits have been discontinued. He does not accumulate vacation time or sick leave, and his employer stops contributions to his pension plan.

Tomás's story is common among Mexican immigrants. Tomás came to the United States from Mexico to work and has been living in the country for three years. A year ago, his wife and two children joined him. Although Tomás works full-time as a kitchen helper in a restaurant, he does not earn enough money to put him above the poverty line. His family struggles from paycheck to paycheck to cover their living expenses. Since Tomás cannot afford to rent his own place, he has to share a two-bedroom apartment with his brother and sister-in-law.

Henry would like to have a steady job, José would like to work more hours, and Tomás would like to earn enough money to adequately provide for his family. Although these three workers are responsible, hardworking men, they have been shortchanged in the labor market—they are underemployed.

Each short life story portrays a different form of underemployment—the unemployed, the part-time employed, and the working poor. Like Henry, the unemployed want to work, but the labor market does not provide enough stable jobs. Henry has not given up looking for work despite a series of unstable jobs. However, his perseverance has not paid off. Joblessness has been a chronic problem among Mexican workers. Since the 1950s, the unemployment rate among Mexicans has been one and a half to two times greater than that among whites, producing fifteen to twenty jobless Mexicans for every ten whites without work (De Anda 1998a; DeFreitas 1991).

Because José often works as few as twenty hours per week, during the rest of the week he is unemployed. Unemployment statistics, however, do not include the partially unemployed. Although José is only partially unemployed, he is not eligible for unemployment insurance benefits. Data from the early 1970s through the 1980s show that Mexicans have been 1.8 to 2.5 times as likely as whites to be involuntary part-time workers (De Anda 1998a).

Tomás's story focuses on the working poor. Even though he works full-time the whole year, his earnings are not higher than the poverty line. This form of underemployment has been widespread during good and bad economic times. For example, the proportion of working poor Mexicans increased between the early 1970s to the late 1980s from 9.5 percent to 13.6 percent (De Anda 1998a). Today, of all other racial/ethnic groups, Latinos are the most likely to be categorized as working poor (U.S. Department of Labor 2002).

Why Study Underemployment?

It is important to study underemployment because people's desire to work, as illustrated in the life stories above, is not being met by the labor market (Clogg, Eliason, and Leicht 2001). Another reason is that the underemployed, on average, have lower earnings than those who are working full-time (De Anda 1998b; Nosal 1998; Zhou 1993). The underemployed are also less likely to have access to fringe benefits such as medical insurance and pension plans (Brown and Yu 2002; de la Torre and Estrada 2001; Tilly 1996). There are also society-wide consequences to underemployment, since inadequate utilization of labor means that the whole society loses potential economic activity. People who could be working and thus productive are not creating wealth. Consequently, society is poorer for it.

In addition to being financially shortchanged, the underemployed experience negative social and psychological effects as well, including declining physical and mental health, higher divorce rates, lower self-esteem, higher incidence of alcoholism and severe depression, increased hopelessness, and more crime (Allen and Steffensmeir 1989; Catalano et al. 2000; Dooley and Prause 1998; Freeman 1996; Prause and Dooley 1997). These social and psychological costs further justify studying underemployment and the importance of understanding its underlying causes.

In this chapter, I compare the causes of underemployment between Mexican-origin and white men. I began by reviewing the literature on personal factors (e.g., education) and job characteristics (e.g., occupation) that have been identified as contributing to joblessness, part-time work, and working poverty. Then I describe the data used for the analysis and the way that variables are measured. This is followed by the presentation of results. I close the chapter with a discussion of the results and suggestions for public policy.

Literature Review

Research shows that the success of workers in the labor market depends on their personal characteristics and the characteristics of the jobs they hold. Personal characteristics—age, education, immigrant status, and ethnicity—influence whether persons are working or not, whether they are working part- or full-time, or whether they are working full-time and earning wages above the poverty level.

A worker's age determines how well he will do in the labor market. In general, young workers do not do as well as older workers in terms of employability and earnings because they have not learned how to look for a job, they have not accumulated work experience, and they are still learning many work-related skills (e.g., punctuality). As a person grows older, he tends to be more experienced in looking for work and has learned more skills while at work (Becker 1993). For these reasons, it is expected that young workers will be more likely to be underemployed than older workers.

Education has been identified as an important variable in predicting workers' employment and how much they will earn. In general, the more education a person has attained, the greater the chances that he will be employed and earn more money than those who have less education (De Anda 1998b). Therefore, it can be anticipated that those workers with lower levels of schooling will face a higher risk of underemployment.

What is the relationship between immigrant status and underemployment? Whether or not someone is born in the United States and the length of time spent living in the country influence the chances of underemployment. Studies show that immigrants' length of residence affects whether they will be underemployed or not. For instance, recent immigrants—those who have lived in the United States for fewer than eleven years—have higher levels of joblessness and part-time work, and they are employed in jobs that pay low wages (De Anda 1992; DeFreitas 1991). This suggests that higher levels of underemployment are expected among recent immigrants compared to those who were born in the United States.

The labor market literature shows that workers' fortunes are also shaped by the type of firm that employs them, since it determines whether or not his job is stable; how much he earns; and whether he works part- or full-time. One of the most important features of a firm is its size—the extent of its assets (e.g., financial resources, buildings, and equipment). Other characteristics that matter are the goods produced (e.g., computers or furniture) or services provided (e.g., banking or janitorial services). How the firm produces those goods or services is also important. The level of the technology used to produce goods or services can be very sophisticated (e.g., making computer chips) or very basic (e.g., making wooden tables). Hence, firms can be grouped into industrial sectors based on *what* they produce and *how* they produce it.

A useful approach that takes these two main characteristics of firms into consideration was developed by Leann Tigges (1987). Using these criteria, she proposed a typology of four industrial sectors: core transformative, periphery transformative, core services, and periphery services.[1] I add the extractive sector because Mexicans tend to be overrepresented in it. Based on this typology, firms in the core tend to be very large, use modern technology, and produce goods and services for national and international markets. On the other hand, firms in the periphery sector tend to be small, use basic technology, and produce for regional or national markets. There are also major differences in the workforce employed by these two sectors. The workforce in periphery firms tends to be unskilled, poorly paid, with few, if any, prospects for advancement. The jobs in these firms tend to be unstable—workers are often employed part-time or are easily laid off. The workforce in core firms is paid higher wages, the jobs are more stable, and workers can count on building a career. Based on these considerations, workers employed in periphery sectors of the economy are more likely to be underemployed than those employed in core sectors of the economy. The exception is the core transformative sector in which workers are susceptible to joblessness.

Occupation influences the chances of underemployment or adequate employment. All jobs have an occupational title based on the worker's duties. For example, a worker can be an accountant, an electrician, or a laborer. Each of these occupations entails a certain level of formal education and/or training. Generally speaking, the higher the level of skill the higher the incumbent's earnings and the more stable the job is likely to be. Persons working in low-skill occupations face higher odds of underemployment than those employed in high-skill occupations.

Data Source

To analyze the causes of underemployment, I use data from the Current Population Survey (CPS). The CPS is a monthly survey conducted by the Department of Commerce for the Bureau of Labor Statistics; it represents the population of the United States (U.S. Bureau of the Census 2000). I use the March 2000 file of the CPS, which contains basic demographic information such as the age and sex of respondents. The survey also includes rich information on the labor market activity of respondents such as employment, whether they are working full- or part-time, occupation, and their annual earnings.

Following the standard practice in studies of labor market activity, the sample is limited to males who were sixteen to sixty-four years of age, not attending school and not in the military or long-term institutions (e.g., those who are incarcerated). Respondents of Mexican descent are those who self-identified as Mexican American, Chicano, Mexican, or Mexicano. These restrictions produced a sample of 3,885 Mexican-origin males and 23,469 white males.

Measurement of Variables

The dependent variable is underemployment; it is measured using the labor utilization framework (LUF) developed by Clogg and Sullivan (1983). The LUF divides the workforce into two categories of workers: the underemployed and a leftover category of adequately employed workers, who work full-time at a wage above the poverty line. The three forms of underemployment used in this chapter are defined as follows:

1. The unemployed refers to persons without a job who are actively looking for one.
2. Involuntary part-time workers includes persons who are working less than thirty-five hours per week but would like to work more; they work few hours due to reasons beyond their control, for example, slack work, shortage in supplies, and breakdowns in plant or equipment.
3. The working poor are people whose annual earnings are less than 1.25 times the poverty line. Thus, in 1999, a person was considered working poor if his earnings were below $10,834, which is the product of the poverty line ($8,667) multiplied by 1.25.

Independent variables are measured as follows. The measurement of age is straightforward. The CPS reports the respondent's age at his or her last birthday. I created several age-groups to capture the effect of age on the likelihood of underemployment: 16–29 years, 30–49 years, and 50–64 years.

Educational attainment is measured with a series of four variables: respondents with up to twelve years of schooling, those with a high school diploma, those with some college, and those with a college degree or higher.

Length of residence in the United States is calculated using information from the CPS item that asks respondents in what year they came to the United States to stay. The following two intervals are constructed: (1) ten years or less and (2) eleven years or more of residence in the United States.

The creation of industrial sectors follows the approach suggested by Tigges (1987): core services, core transformative, periphery services, and periphery transformative. The categorization of industrial sectors employs the standard industry classification three-digit code for industry provided in the survey for each respondent's current or most recent job.

Occupational categories are based on the two-digit detailed recodes provided in the survey. The occupation corresponds to the respondent's current or last job. Six occupational categories are used in the analysis: administrators and professionals; technical, sales, and administrative support; services; precision production, craft, and repair; operatives and assemblers; and laborers and farmworkers.

Method of Analysis

The data analysis is organized into two parts. The first part presents descriptive statistics for the variables used in the analysis. It compares the percentage distribution of underemployed Mexican and white males, as well as the distribution of independent variables (e.g., personal characteristics—age and education; job characteristics—industry and occupation). The second part of the analysis uses logistic regression. The dependent variable has two categories: underemployed or adequately employed workers (i.e., full-time work). The logistic model predicts underemployment using the independent variables discussed. I estimate separate models for Mexican and white workers. The odds ratios in the logistic model are interpreted as the factor—a multiplicative effect—by which an independent variable affects the chances that a person will be underemployed (for a useful introduction to logistic regression, see Lottes, Adler, and DeMaris 1996).

Results of Analysis

The Prevalence of Underemployment

Table 2.1 shows the percentage distribution of underemployed Mexican-origin and white males. Mexican workers were underemployed more than twice as often as white workers: 22.4 percent and 10.5 percent, respectively. Of the three forms of underemployment, the most easily recognized is joblessness. Yet joblessness had the smallest gap between Mexican and white workers—a ratio of 1.7. That is, there were seventeen jobless Mexican workers for every ten whites without work. The widest gap between Mexican and white males was concerning working poverty with a Mexican-to-white ratio of 2.4, which is equivalent to twenty-four working poor Mexicans to ten whites. Thus, working poverty is the most severe form of underemployment for Mexican males. In fact, for Mexicans, working poverty is more than half of their total underemployment (13.5/22.4 = 60.3 percent).

TABLE 2.1
Percentage of Underemployed Mexican and White Males

	Unemployed	Involuntary Part-Time	Working Poor	Total Underemployed
Mexican	5.3	3.6	13.5	22.4
White	3.1	1.8	5.6	10.5
Ratio	1.7	2.0	2.4	2.1

Descriptive Profile

Table 2.2 reports descriptive measures of personal and job characteristics of Mexican and white males in the sample. The results confirm that young workers of Mexican descent were more likely to be active in the labor force than white workers. Over one-third of Mexican men were in the sixteen- to twenty-nine-year-old group, compared to about one-fourth of their white counterparts. The pattern was reversed for Mexican and white workers in the oldest age-group (45–64): Mexican workers were about one-fifth, while white workers were a little over one-third.

Mexican men were disadvantaged in terms of educational attainment relative to white men. Nearly half (48.3 percent) of Mexican-origin men had twelve years or less of schooling, whereas less than one-tenth (9.5 percent) of white men had such low levels of attainment. This large educational gap is due in part to the preponderance of immigrants, who tend to have lower levels of schooling compared to those born in the United States. The good news is that the high school completion gap between Mexicans and whites seems to be narrowing—the corresponding graduation rates were 28.6 percent and 31.2 percent. Unfortunately, college graduation rates remained dismally low for Mexicans (6.1 percent) relative to whites (30.8 percent).

A significant characteristic of Mexican-origin male workers is that more than half of them were born in Mexico. This reflects the increase of emigrants leaving Mexico to work in the United States in the past couple of decades. Of the total Mexican-origin workforce, close to one-quarter (23.7 percent) were recent arrivals—had lived in the United States less than eleven years. More than one-third (36.3 percent) had lived in the United States for at least eleven years.

Mexican men were more often employed in industrial sectors with jobs that exposed them to a high risk of underemployment. Compared to white males, Mexican workers were often underrepresented in industrial sectors that would protect them from underemployment. The core services sector should shield workers from employment hardship. Unfortunately, there were nearly half as many Mexican men (12 percent) as white men (22 percent) employed in this sector. Not surprisingly, Mexican men were disproportionately employed in the extractive sector compared to white men: 11.9 percent and 3.4 percent, respectively.

Due to their occupational distribution, Mexicans, compared to white workers, were disadvantaged in the labor market. Mexican workers were severely underrepresented in white-collar, skilled occupations (e.g., professionals and

TABLE 2.2
Descriptive Statistics

	Mexican	White
Age-Group		
16–29 years	38.6	24.4
30–44 years	41.7	40.3
45–64 years	19.7	35.3
Education		
12 years or less	48.3	9.5
High school diploma	28.6	31.7
Some college	17.0	28.1
College degree or higher	6.1	30.7
Length of Residence		
10 years or less	23.7	1.5
11 years or more	36.3	3.5
U.S.-born	40.0	95.5
Industrial Sector		
Core transformative	32.2	30.1
Core services	12.3	22.4
Periphery transformative	4.8	3.6
Periphery services	38.8	40.5
Extractive	11.9	3.4
Occupation		
Admin. and professional	8.9	31.6
Technical, sales, adm., support	12.4	20.4
Services	14.7	8.7
Precision production, craft, repair	23.6	19.2
Machine operators, assemblers	17.6	12.4
Laborers, farmworkers	22.8	7.7
N	3,885	23,469

Note: The sample size is unweighted, but tabulations were weighted.

administrators). This is detrimental to Mexican workers. Since these occupations pay the highest wages and tend to be the most stable, they protect workers from underemployment. Mexicans were disproportionately concentrated in occupations associated with a high risk of underemployment: over three-fourths were employed in services, blue-collar, laborer, and farmworker occupations. In contrast, less than half of white workers were similarly employed. This skewed occupational distribution is in part a reflection of Mexican men's lower than average schooling levels.

Causes of Underemployment

Table 2.3 displays the results of the logistic models predicting the odds that a worker will be underemployed (for coefficients and standard errors, see appendix 2.1). The models are estimated separately for Mexican and white males. For Mexican men, the risk of underemployment was highest for young, poorly educated, recent immigrants employed in periphery-like industrial sectors and low-skilled occupations.

More specifically, the results show that Mexican men between the ages of sixteen and twenty-nine were slightly more vulnerable to be underemployed relative to white men. The results for education were more telling, however. The lack of education renders Mexican workers susceptible to underemployment. For example, poorly educated Mexican men (i.e., those with twelve or less years of schooling) were 2.1 times more likely to be underemployed. But

TABLE 2.3
Logistic Models Predicting Underemployment (odds ratios)

	Mexican	White
Age-Group		
16–29 years	1.66**	1.64***
30–44 years	1.15	0.94
Education		
12 years or less	2.05*	1.88***
High school diploma	1.44	1.49***
Some college	0.86	1.17*
Length of Residence		
10 years or less	1.57**	1.18
11 years or more	1.18	1.31*
Industrial Sector		
Core transformative	1.61*	1.51***
Periphery transformative	1.58	1.36*
Periphery services	1.74**	1.92***
Extractive	2.61***	2.59***
Occupation		
Technical, sales, adm., support	2.88***	1.36***
Services	1.97*	1.96***
Precision production, craft, repair	2.30**	1.83***
Machine operators, assemblers	1.96*	1.89***
Laborers, farmworkers	2.98***	3.48***
N	3,885	23,469

*p ≤ .05, **p ≤ .01, ***p ≤ .001

white males with the same level of schooling were only 1.9 times as likely to be underemployed. The odds of underemployment are lower for whites with a high school diploma compared to their peers without a high school diploma. Such a relationship does not attain for Mexicans with a high school diploma; in fact, the results are not statistically significant.

Recent Mexican immigrants (i.e., those who lived in the United States for less than 11 years) were 1.6 times more likely to be underemployed than their peers who were born in the United States. Mexican immigrants who lived in the United States for eleven or more years had no greater or lesser chance to be underemployed than their peers who were born in this country. In other words, Mexican immigrants remain at risk of underemployment during the first ten years of residence in the United States. After that, the immigrants' chances to be underemployed are not statistically different from those who were born in the United States.

In terms of industrial sector employment, Mexican workers in the extractive sector (i.e., agriculture, forestry, and fisheries) face the highest odds of underemployment. This is not surprising since agricultural jobs tend to be poorly paid and unstable. This finding is important because nearly 12 percent of Mexican-origin males are employed in this sector, whereas less than 4 percent of white males are similarly employed. Mexicans employed in the core transformative sector were also vulnerable to underemployment to a greater extent than their white counterparts. This is significant because nearly one-third of all Mexican workers were employed in this sector.

The type of occupation that Mexican workers hold has a strong effect on the odds of underemployment. As was hypothesized, the results show that workers in low-skilled occupations were the least protected from underemployment. Mexican laborers and farmworkers were nearly three (2.9) times more likely than their coethnics employed in administrative and professional occupations to be underemployed. It was anticipated that employment in skilled occupations would protect workers from underemployment. This was not the case for Mexicans employed in precision production, craft, and repair occupations. Mexicans in those occupations were 2.3 times as likely to be underemployed, compared to 1.8 times for white workers—Mexican workers were 50 percent more likely than white workers to be underemployed. Why is this so? Possibly Mexican workers in these occupations do not belong to labor unions, which would offer protection from joblessness, part-time work, and working poverty. The other possibility is that they are the first to be laid off whenever the economy slows down. More important, these results suggest that Mexican workers are discriminated against even when they have the necessary skills to obtain higher-paying, stable jobs.

Conclusion

This chapter compared the causes of underemployment between Mexican-origin and white men. The underemployed were persons whose willingness to work was not satisfied in the labor market or who were working full-time but living in poverty. The results clearly show that Mexican workers were short-changed in the labor market to a greater extent than white workers: Mexican workers were underemployed more than twice as often as their white counterparts. The highest risk of underemployment for Mexicans was found among those who were young and poorly educated, those who were recent immigrants, and those employed in periphery industrial sectors and unskilled occupations.

The results indicate that the most prevalent form of underemployment is working poverty. In fact, working poverty makes up more than half of all Mexican underemployment. This is in part a consequence of working in low-skilled jobs that pay very low wages. There are several ways in which the labor market outcomes of workers in low-wage occupations can be improved. One way is by increasing the education level of Mexican workers. This would reduce the risk of underemployment. It would also channel Mexicans into more stable, better-paying jobs. Therefore, parents and educators should encourage young men to stay in school and graduate. The Mexican community should keep demanding that schools set up programs that prevent students from dropping out and help them graduate.

On the public policy front, efforts should be directed at increasing the federal minimum wage. Although there has been much resistance to this change, many cities and states have been able to raise the local minimum wage above the federally mandated minimum. For example, the current federally mandated minimum is $5.15 per hour, but several states have higher statewide minimum wages—California ($6.75), Oregon ($7.05), and Washington ($7.01) (U.S. Department of Labor 2004).

Another way to improve the wages of the working poor is by establishing local living wage ordinances. Living wage ordinances take into consideration the cost of living in a particular city or county. Although these ordinances only benefit workers employed by businesses that rely on public money, it is a step in the right direction. The following cities, for example, have instituted living wage ordinances: Fairfax, California ($13.00), San Jose, California ($10.10), and Chicago, Illinois ($9.05) (ACORN 2003). Fiscal policy can also be implemented to improve the living conditions of the working poor by reducing the tax burden on their wages. This is a tax policy that allows workers with low earnings to receive a refund from the federal government when the credit exceeds the income taxes owed. By increasing the current earned income tax credit, the working poor could keep a greater proportion of their wages.

The likelihood of underemployment would be minimized if workers joined labor unions. Unions are instrumental in keeping their members working and helping them find suitable employment when they are not working. Unionized workers receive better wages and have access to better fringe benefits than those who are not organized. For example, unionized workers are more likely than unorganized workers to have medical insurance and pension plans.

Although involuntary part-time workers are partially unemployed, they are not eligible to receive unemployment insurance benefits. They do not choose to be partially unemployed; rather, their employers reduced the number of hours available for work. To minimize the loss of income among involuntary part-time workers, they should be able to receive unemployment insurance benefits.

The results also suggest that recent immigrants had a higher likelihood of underemployment compared to their peers born in the United States. This is not due to joblessness, since Mexican men migrate to the United States primarily to work. Recent immigrants' higher rate of underemployment is the result of the unstable low-wage jobs that they are likely to accept in the first few years of living in this country. Another reason is that recent immigrants are also more likely to be employed part-time compared to those who have lived longer in the United States (De Anda 1992). The results show that underemployment for immigrants is a temporary situation; after they live in the United States for ten years, their labor market fortunes improve—they get stable, better-paying jobs. In short, the higher levels of underemployment among Mexican-origin workers relative to whites cannot be attributed to immigrants alone.

In this chapter the process that leads to underemployment was examined separately for Mexicans and whites. The results show that personal and job characteristics do not offer Mexicans the same protection from underemployment that white workers have. For instance, in each occupational category Mexicans were more prone to be underemployed than their white counterparts. This suggests that Mexican workers are treated less favorably in the labor market compared to white workers. To eliminate discrimination in the labor market, equal employment opportunity laws should be strengthened and enforced. If measures are not taken to reduce the prevalence of underemployment, then Mexican workers, as well as the larger society, will continue to be shortchanged.

Note

I would like to thank Michael Sobczak for computing assistance.

1. Tigges's (1987) typology of economic sectors includes the following typical firms: *core transformative*—construction, food products, and transportation equipment; *core services*—air transportation, banking, and finance; *periphery transformative*—furniture and fixtures, textile mill products; *periphery services*—transportation, wholesale trade, and repair services. The *extractive* sector includes agriculture, forestry, fisheries, and mining.

References

ACORN. 2003. Association of Community Organizations for Reform Now. Living Wage Resource Center. www.livingwagecampaign.org.

Allen, E., and D. Steffensmeir. 1989. "Youth, Underemployment, and Property Crime: Differential Effects of Job Stability and Job Quality on Juvenile and Young Adult Arrest Rates." *American Sociological Review* 54: 107–23.

Becker, Gary S. 1993. *Human Capital.* 3d ed. Chicago: University of Chicago Press.

Brown, Richard E., and Hongjian Yu. 2002. "Latinos' Access to Employment-Based Health Insurance." In *Latinos: Remaking America*, ed. Marcelo M. Suarez-Orozco and Mariela M. Paez, 236–53. Berkeley: University of California Press.

Catalano, Ralph, Ethel Aldrete, William Vega, Bohdan Kolody, and Sergio Aguilar-Gaxiola. 2000. "Job Loss and Major Depression among Mexican Americans." *Social Science Quarterly* 81, no. 1: 477–87.

Clogg, Clifford C., Scott R. Eliason, and Kevin T. Leicht. 2001. *Analyzing the Labor Force: Concepts, Measures, and Trends.* New York: Kluwer Academic/Plenum.

Clogg, Clifford C., and Teresa Sullivan. 1983. "Labor Force Composition and Underemployment Trends, 1969–1980." *Social Indicators Research* 12: 117–52.

De Anda, Roberto M. 1998a. "Labor-Force Inequality of Mexican-Origin Workers." In *Race and Ethnicity in the United States: An Institutional Approach*, ed. William Velez, 178–91. Dix Hills, NY: General Hall.

———. 1998b. "Employment Instability and Earnings of Mexican-Origin Men." *Hispanic Journal of Behavioral Sciences* 20, no. 3: 363–74.

———. 1994. "Unemployment and Underemployment among Mexican-Origin Workers." *Hispanic Journal of Behavioral Sciences* 16: 163–75.

———. 1992. "Involuntary Part-Time Work among Chicanos: Its Causes and Consequences." In *Chicano Discourse*, ed. Tatcho Mindiola and Emilio Zamora, 69–87. Houston: Mexican American Studies Program, University of Houston.

DeFreitas, Gregory. 1991. *Inequality at Work: Hispanics in the U.S. Labor Force.* New York: Oxford University Press.

de la Torre, Adela, and Antonio Estrada. 2001. *Mexican Americans and Health.* Tucson: University of Arizona Press.

Dooley, David, and JoAnn Prause. 1998. "Underemployment and Alcohol Misuse in the National Longitudinal Survey of Youth." *Journal of Studies on Alcohol* 59, no. 6: 669–80.

Freeman, Richard B. 1996. "Why Do So Many Young American Men Commit Crimes and What We Might Do about It?" *Journal of Economic Perspectives* 10, no. 1: 25–42.

Lottes, Ilsa A., Marina A. Adler, and Alfred DeMaris. 1996. "Using and Interpreting Logistic Regression: A Guide for Teachers and Students." *Teaching Sociology* 24: 284–98.

Nosal, Ed. 1998. "Financial Distress and Underemployment." *Review of Economic Studies* 65, no. 4: 817–45.

Prause, JoAnn, and David Dooley. 1997. "Effect of Underemployment on School-Leavers Self-Esteem." *Journal of Adolescence* 20, no. 3: 243–60.

Tigges, Leann M. 1987. *Changing Fortunes: Industrial Sectors and Workers' Earnings.* New York: Praeger.

Tilly, Chris. 1996. *Half a Job: Bad and Good Part-Time Jobs in a Changing Labor Market.* Philadelphia: Temple University Press.

U.S. Bureau of the Census. 2000. Current Population Survey: Annual Demographic File, 2000. Machine-readable data file. ICPSR version. Washington, D.C.: U.S. Bureau of the Census (producer). Ann Arbor, MI: Inter-University Consortium for Political and Social Research (distributor).

U.S. Department of Labor. 2002. *A Profile of the Working Poor, 2000.* Bureau of Labor Statistics. Report 957. www.bls.gov/cps/cpswp2000.htm.

———. 2004. www.dol.gov/esa/minwage/american.htm.

Zhou, M. 1993. "Underemployment and Economic Disparities among Minority Groups." *Population Research and Policy Review* 12: 139–57.

APPENDIX 2.1
Logistic Regression Models Predicting Underemployment

	Mexican			White		
	b	(s.e.)	Exp(b)	b	(s.e.)	Exp(b)
Age-Group						
16–29 years	0.509**	(.157)	1.66	0.496***	(.061)	1.64
30–44 years	0.144	(.152)	1.15	−0.063	(.058)	0.94
45–64 years [reference]						
Education						
12 years or less	0.718*	(.311)	2.05	0.633***	(.086)	1.88
High school diploma	0.365	(.312)	1.44	0.397***	(.074)	1.49
Some college	-0.149	(.328)	0.86	0.155*	(.074)	1.17
College degree [reference]						
Length of Residence						
10 years or less	0.450***	(.134)	1.57	0.166	(.166)	1.18
11 years or more	0.167	(.131)	1.18	0.268*	(.118)	1.31
U.S.-born [reference]						
Industrial Sector						
Core transformative	0.475*	(.215)	1.61	0.415***	(.078)	1.51
Core services [reference]						
Periphery transformative	0.455	(.215)	1.58	0.311*	(.132)	1.36
Periphery services	0.552**	(.207)	1.74	0.653***	(.071)	1.92
Extractive	0.958***	(.242)	2.61	0.950***	(.114)	2.59
Occupation						
Admin. and professional[reference]						
Technical, sales, adm., support	1.059***	(.305)	2.88	0.310***	(.078)	1.36
Services	0.678*	(.306)	1.97	0.675***	(.090)	1.96
Precision production, craft, repair	0.831**	(.302)	2.30	0.603***	(.082)	1.83
Machine operators, assemblers	0.675*	(.307)	1.96	0.638***	(.089)	1.89
Laborers, farmworkers	1.091***	(.302)	2.98	1.248***	(.089)	3.48
Intercept	−3.198***			−3.133***		
-2 Log likelihood	2618.614			14915.438		
N	3,885			23,469		

*p ≤ .05, **p ≤ .01, ***p ≤ .001

PART II

ETHNIC IDENTITY FORMATION AND EDUCATION: THE EXPERIENCES OF CHILDREN AND TEACHERS

3

Learning *Manito* Discourse: Children's Stories and Identity in Northern New Mexico

Eric Romero

YOUNG BRIANA (AGE 10) PREFACES THE FOLLOWING NARRATIVE by stating that it took her "all weekend." Before reading to the fifth grade class, she thanks everyone who helped with suggestions and support. Her prefacing comments are all in English, but she transitions quickly to a Spanish/English code-switching mode (using more than one language in sentence construction) once she begins to read:

> I live in a beautiful *valle* (valley). In the *valle* where I live, there is my house way back in the *bosque*. In the ranch I have two *gatos*. Their names are Skipper and Stinker. I also have *tres perros. Sus nombres son* Boots, Spots, and Rosa. *Son muy buenos perros.*
>
> *En mi rancho tenemos venaos y alasanes.* We hunt them for food. We sometimes make *carne seca, que es muy vuena.* We also hunt turkey *y gallinas de la Sierra.*
>
> *En mi valle tambien viven osos y coyotes.* We have to be especially careful *con los osos que estan muy ambrientos. Los coyotes* are afraid of us and usually run away.
>
> *Los pajaros en mi valle son grandes y pequenos y muy bonitos.* They chirp very beautiful.
>
> *En mi valle,* I have to work very hard. On my *rancho* we brand cows, ride horses, and gather *todas las bacas.* We use *una baca para leche. Mi caballo se llama Whiskey.* The others are Mayo, the buckskin, and the Apalusa *se llama Wapo. Que bonitos son mis caballos. Mi padre y mi tio amansan caballos* for roping *y erando la bacas,* and also *pa pasiarnos en lleos. Los arboles y todas las plantas y flores en mi valle son muy bonitas y hermosas.* They smell so good.
>
> The *rio que corre por mi valle* is very nice. *En el rio se puede ver pez.* Sometimes I fish with my dad and uncle. *A la tarde* we have a fish fry for all my family.
>
> *La iglesia en mi valle* is small and pretty. *Es la iglesia de San Jose. Mis padres se casaron en esta iglesita de mi valle. Es la iglesia* where I pray to Jesus, thank Jesus, and also confess to Jesus.

Mi escuela es pequena y esta en Sapello, which is also part of my *valle. Tengo muchos amigos, y amigas que van* with mi to school. Some old houses are still standing that were built buy a lot of our grandparents. There were built of *adobe y vigas.* Some people have restored some of these old houses. In the *night mi valle es muy hermosa tambien.* My family and I sometimes sit on the porch *pa ver la luna y las estrellas. Ay que bonito y hermoso es mi valle. El Fin.* (For a translation, see the appendix at the end of this chapter.)

Introduction

Bien aprende quien buen maestro tiene (One will learn well with a good teacher)

Briana's story demonstrates the kind of verbal strategies and content that are common with many Chicano children and youth growing up in the mountain villages of northern New Mexico.[1] It is a "way of speaking" found in many contexts of home and community—a conversational style that helps community members share information, support social relationships, and identify cultural similarities. Participation in these conversations requires certain styles of speaking and structuring of narratives. This way of speaking reflects deeper understandings of language use, group identification, and social contexts. These language strategies also provide an understanding of common subsistence skills and a shared reverence for the natural environment. Children in many villages learn to use these language and narrative skills to demonstrate their affinity to communities that have developed strong ties to land and community. At a more developed level these language skills are used as a response to larger societal forces that continue to impact local culture, language, and life practices.

These narrative skills are not inherent to general strategies for speech acquisition; rather, they reflect language socialization strategies that occur in a variety of social contexts. These language strategies can be facilitated, negotiated, or stifled by the different social institutions to which these children are exposed. One of these institutions is the public school system, which has the capacity either to hear these stories or to silence them in formal learning situations.

This chapter takes a look at language socialization and language use strategies that reflect a deeper cultural understanding of Hispanic village life. It will demonstrate a relationship between language socialization processes, particularly related to narrative structuring, and the development of "place identity" among Hispanic inhabitants of select mountain villages in northern New Mexico.[2] This work suggests a conceptualization for place identity that contributes to our understanding of self-identity and ethnic-identity formation.

To understand more about these linguistic skills it is necessary to become familiar with the historical and regional contexts for local language socialization where this learning takes place. The historical development of village populations must also be taken into account, including the formation of village culture and the contemporary struggles for survival in a harsh mountain environment.

This chapter draws from an ongoing anthropological research project in the geographical area described below, an applied social science project with prospective importance to rural education, curriculum design, and community development applications. The analysis portion of the chapter will be accompanied with suggestions for application in different fields.

Research Methodology

La necesidad es madre de la habilidad (Necessity is mother to skill)

The primary strategy of this ethnographic research project is to identify patterns in language use that can be used to identify how Chicano children learn to become members of local community and culture. Children learn a "way of speaking" that helps them become members of a discursive community that shares cultural information and subsistence knowledge. It is necessary to identify naturally occurring language use and narrative formation that reflects the development of individual character. It is also necessary to identify language use that can be attributed to language socialization practices of home and school. To do this requires an understanding of the different contexts and contents where particular reference points relating to children's knowledge and discussion of place are found.

I spent more than five years gathering data from school and community environments. I began the ethnographic research with data taken from children in a variety of contexts, including school lunchrooms, classrooms, and buses. I obtained much of this information from children riding the four bus routes that serve the many villages in the Sapello area. This strategy turned out to be useful to acquire children's narratives and oral descriptions of physical features of the local communities. I also conducted many interviews with children and parents in their homes, getting a better understanding of what household conversations entailed. The narratives provided information regarding local cultural activity, recreation opportunities, community events, and household subsistence activities. Briana's story is indicative of the types of themes that children speak of. Her story speaks about recreational and family activities and describes the subsistence activities of hunting, ranching, and home construction.

As a second level of data collection, I procured student schoolwork from classroom activities. This data collection focused on written and oral narratives of place as presented in the classrooms. The story provided above is an example from this level of data collection. This level of data was necessary to develop the understanding of narrative construction in formal education settings and the ability of education strategies to access deeper levels of student knowledge.

Village Formation

Ama a tu projimo como a ti mismo (Love your neighbor as you love yourself)

To comprehend the importance of place and community in these children's narratives it is necessary to understand the formation of village culture. Some villages can claim a four-century colonization history extending back to the original Spanish *entrada* into the area. Since early colonization, the general pattern for colonial settlement reflected more the necessity to be close to farmlands and water irrigation systems rather than a convenient centralization for civil, military, and clerical authorities (Swadesh 1974). The Spanish and Mexican colonization process in these areas followed a pattern of ecological legitimacy in which importance was placed on land conservation strategies for community survival (Pena 1998). This form of community planning is characteristic of the *mercedes* (land grant) system of land distribution and colonization and is based on an economy of subsistence agriculture and "vertical transhumance grazing" of livestock (Pulido 1998, 122). This pastoral strategy utilizes the differences of environmental zones and seasonal cycles for domesticated animal pasturing and the planting of foodstuffs.

The first Hispanic colonizers to arrive in the region recognized the importance of collecting and distributing water to irrigate their farms. Native Americans in the region had already created elaborate water distribution systems for their farming. Built on the experience of both Native American and Middle Eastern technologies, the *acequia* system was established in northern New Mexico.

Subsistence and Environment

Agua que no haz de beber, dejala correr (Water that you do not drink, let it flow)

Many contemporary village behaviors still make reference to colonial village formation and cultural geography, particularly in relation to the use of natural resources. The importance of the resources from the Sangre de Cristo Mountains cannot be underestimated for the sustainability of northern New Mexico villages. The most precious of these mountain resources is water.

Acequia refers to the community-designed irrigation ditches that warrant the planting of foodstuffs and forage, as well as the organizational structure of the respective farmers who benefit from the constructed system. Creating and maintaining the system required the whole community to commit to a common effort. People had to establish and abide by rules directing the use of the system and the water it carried, as well as participate in the governing and management roles required to coordinate the use of the system for all aspects of the community.

The community participation, governance, and ecological practices established by the *acequia* system continue to influence communities today. The maintenance of *acequia* organizations is critical to the shared heritage and communal ethic of villagers. Because of the prevalence of *acequia* irrigation practices, many communities practice an institutionalized orientation toward land stewardship and water conservation. These shared concerns find their way into many daily discussions and can be used as a measure of one's familiarity and affinity to their respective communities.

Children learn to speak of *acequias* from a position of divergent meanings. This shared discussion of communal water, community organization, and created ecosystems is the cultural patrimony of these small villages. Examples of these levels of meaning are identifiable in the following poem written by third grader Stacy:

> the *acequia* brings us water
> the *acequia* brings us life
> we work to clean the *acequia*
> and plant are plants
> we can swim in the *acequia*
> and have fun there

Contemporary Villages

Cuando llego el alambre vino el hambre (When the fences came so did hunger)

The most profound impact on New Mexico village life has been the transition from Mexican government to U.S. government, which is based on a different understanding of land tenure. During this transition most land grant communities lost significant communal land holdings.

The Great Depression was an important time for New Mexico's villages. The federal government's concern for rural assistance programs and reform programs had an impact on the area with repercussions extending far into the future. William deBuys introduces Suzanne Forrest's book on the period by stating, "Perhaps no other period *(great depression)* so emphatically shapes the present, for it was during the New Deal years that the region underwent the most intense and excruciating transition in its recent history" (Forrest 1989). Forrest goes on to explain, "In the process of coping with the Anglo-introduced forces of economic and technological change, they [New Mexicans] adapted new tactics for their economic and technological change" (Forrest 1989). Some of these survival strategies included people taking part in migrant labor in urban areas or working in industries such as railroad construction, mining, commercial agriculture, or outside ranching operations. This was primarily a male phenomenon but families were also moved to urban areas that are now presented with third- and fourth-generation *manito*-origin communities. In another survival strategy, many cultural behaviors became more entrenched and necessary for village survival. Consequently, outside hegemonic influences helped strengthen the subsistence practices of villages and allowed for the creation of more cohesion among villagers.

Hispanic villages in the mountains and valleys of northern New Mexico and southern Colorado are beset with the contradictions and diverse phenomena of other rural areas. They are blessed with the vestiges of traditional rural lifestyles but also benefit from twenty-first-century conveniences. These mountain communities continue to be populated mostly by families representing an Indo-Hispano land-based village culture.

Present-day subsistence and cultural practices reflect a variety of strategies mixing traditional and contemporary knowledge. Many isolated villages still reflect land-based subsistence practices that historically helped the communities survive the harsh mountain environment that defined the northern boundaries of the Spanish and Mexican governments. These practices, as well as related commercial opportunities, are closely tied to the mountain environment and the utilization of natural resources. Some domestic practices, such as family gardens and foodstuff preservation, have remained essential and unchanged for centuries. Families still rely on fishing, hunting, and gathering to supplement their diets. As in the past, many homes are heated by wood-burning stoves, and woodcutting is an important chore. Many families augment their household income with the sale of trees, firewood, and stone, as well as livestock. Seasonal cycles are very important to determining daily household chores and activities. Families often collaborate on projects reflecting a communal orientation to task accomplishments. Many children are familiar with their responsibility to help clean the *acequia* or to share produce from gardens. Due to the long-established structures for common natural resource utilization and community collaboration, villagers maintained a powerful sense of place and adherence to principles of land stewardship.

Children who are raised in these villages are presented with the option of adherence to community-level concerns for preservation of heritage and subsistence behaviors conflated with the increasing awareness of the world outside of their own. They are instructed to value the practices and opportunities that accompany living on the mountain slopes. They are also familiarized with the benefits of fast-paced urban living. Because of these inherent paradoxes, it becomes increasingly important to look critically at the kinds of institutions that may have sway with these modernizing influences. Schools help children navigate external and community-based influences and ultimately have a bearing on the individual's understanding of ethnicity and self.

Ethnic Identity and Place

Dime con quien andas y te dire quien eres (Tell me with whom you are accompanied and I will tell you who you are)

Like many concepts utilized for descriptive and analytical purposes, the concept of ethnicity is not an exacting or agreed-on criterion. There are many views of the meaning and complexities of ethnicity as a social construct. I will not develop a full sociological discussion of ethnicity but will rely on some heuristic considerations as they relate to the subject of this chapter. Ethnicity in a general sense can be considered a shared system of codes that give meaning, identity, and sense of belonging, creating boundaries that distinguish one group from another (Arizpe 1992). This dynamic between different cultural groups has to be understood from a perspective of the historical processes that lend for differences and formed identities. These historical processes also help us understand the superordinate/subordinate power relations that underlie ethnic relations (Melville 1983). In this sense ethnicity is also understood as a power relationship between groups that have developed through historical processes. Ethnic identity and ingroup/outgroup distinctions reflect processes that determine otherness and consequently self-identity. Keefe summarizes, "Affiliation with a particular ethnic group and culture is the sum of each individual's experience interacting with members of various ethnic groups and the individual's evaluation of these personal experiences and the ethnic perceptions and attitudes of others" (Keefe 1992, 36). This means that ascription to particular groups is a relationship of personal identity and affinity with others.

Bioregionalism and *Querencia* of Place

El que pierde su tierra pierde su memoria (He who loses his land loses his memory)

In this chapter I suggest conceptualization of place identity as an additional tool to help understand the realities of regional ethnic identity. This concept is particularly useful for land-based cultures that incorporate place knowledge into their schema for ethnicity. Place identity is particularly useful in explorations of ethnic group orientations of place and identity and more relevant with reference to the land-based Chicano population of New Mexico villages.

The concept of place identity draws from several disciplines. This reflects the more general question of the individual's awareness of landscape and community. Discussion in the areas of human geography (Foucault 1980; Harvey 1996), environmental psychology (Gifford 1987), behavioral archaeology (Zedeno 2000), border studies (Gonzalez 2001; Velez-Ibanez 1997), and linguistic anthropology (Rodman 1992; Basso 1996; Hirsch and O'Hanlon 1995) have contributed to our understanding of cultural conceptualizations of place, landscape, and community.

I propose place identity as an additional level of understanding that we can use to comprehend the complex relationships of culture and identity for the *manito* village populations of northern New Mexico. This *manito* identity has its cohesive effects not only on the community internally but also in the outside world. *Manito* respect for fellow villagers and ancestral land finds incarnation in several community concepts. For example, Esteban Arellano identifies the concept of *querencia* to explain this deep-felt affinity to the land: "That communion with the landscape ties us to the enduring code of brotherhood just as the poet makes the landscape itself the carrier of memory" (Arellano 1997, 31). *Querencia* is an affection and respect for a special place that translates into a responsibility to care for that place (Atencio 2001). Northern New Mexico villagers use *querencia* as a common discourse to exchange knowledge of environmental and subsistence practices as part of daily discussions. This discursive sharing bonds villagers to community and region.

Young Briana begins to explore her affinity to place and community by speaking to the beauty of the valley and the smell of flowers and plants. She also speaks of the importance of recognizing the older buildings built by family elders. The use of these discourse strategies demonstrates that Briana is coming to recognize the deeper significance of environment and place.

Another example that sheds light on the complex relationship of environment and subsistence can be found in a short story by fourth grader Tazianne:

One night when me and my mom were at Walmart we were coming out and saw a mountain lion on the back of a truck but it was dead. The guy shot it I thought poor thing because it was a mother and it had babies but the babies were still in the den. The mother mountain lion had blood coming from her side it was all over her. What I guessed is that she was going after their horses. So he shot her and di'nt even think if she had babies or anything and in some ways I think it was cruel.

This story assigns value to an animal's life and recognizes the possible repercussions of the hunter's actions. It also suggests a very real scenario—the lion may have been threatening livestock. These situations and judgments reflect a relationship with the natural environment that is based on stewardship, subsistence, and community virtues. It is a relationship that changes constantly but is also centered on long-standing appreciation taught to children and youth.

This ethno-philosophy for land stewardship and community integrity is a relatively new discussion for Chicano studies scholars. Devon Pena posits the urgency to develop an understanding for "truth in-place" that recognizes regional ecology as an "unstable and shifting mosaic" rather than a "stable climax community" (Pena 1998). He presents the potential of bioregional study for its ability to contradict "hegemonic" Western ideas on conservation but also identifies its usefulness for an understanding of identity. *Querencia*, bioregional study, and place identity can promote fuller comprehension of the complexities of Chicano populations. These concepts can clarify our understanding of the regional differences of a heterogeneous population that is too often portrayed as an urban phenomenon.

To access these insights into place, stewardship, and community affinity we must use research methods that can take us to cultural and ideological understandings of our subject populations. There are many mechanisms that can help us, the most valuable being linguistic material.

Language and Cultural Expression

De las palabras: no el sonido, sino el sentido (About words: not the sound, but the meaning)

Linguistic analysis can provide substantial insight into issues of cultural importance. There are many levels of analysis that can be used to investigate cultural processes, some more illuminating than others. The areas of language research and analysis employed in this section are at a sociocultural level of understanding rather than an analysis of language structuring (phonology, morphology). The selected general strategies of discourse analysis and narrative analysis provide the insights necessary to comprehend the process of cultural transmission and identity formation relevant to an understanding of place. The determination of these areas of analysis is closely related to their ability to demonstrate cultural and personal insights from the data. These levels of analysis provide a holistic understanding of how the villagers and children come to conceptualize their relationship with the environment and with one another.

Some specific discourse strategies occur in the code-switching strategies that emphasize particular "power" concepts that do not translate readily. Children learn to use Spanish words like *acequia, sierra* (mountain range), *carne seca* (meat jerky), *mayordomo* (*acequia* boss), and *ojo* (artesian spring) because of the cultural meaning attached to their usage. Children may know the English equivalent to these words, but they also understand that the translated version does not adequately reflect the deeper cultural significance. Briana's narrative and Stacy's poem demonstrate code-switching strategies to emphasize words that carry a cultural significance. Although children may be familiar with the English equivalents of many of these Spanish words, it is not common for them to use the translation. Another area where children used much Spanish language is in reference to extended family relationships *(tio, tia, nana, abuelito, nino)*.

Spanish/English code-switching is less common in children's speech than in adult speech. Children exercise more code-switching strategies when adults are present. In the solicited narratives provided on bus rides and on school grounds children characteristically responded in English even when suggested to use other terminology. At home there tended to be much more code-switching, particularly with important lexical features such as geographical features and place-names.

Another common discourse strategy is for children to speak of relationships with animals, both domestic and wild. Briana speaks of riding horses for roping and herding activities as well as enjoyment. In speaking of domestic animals children learn to suggest a partnership for mutual benefit. They often address these animals as allies and wards. They speak of the moral, collegial, and economical responsibilities to care for an animal. They often address the loss of an animal as similar to the loss of a family member. Briana and Taziana also speak of hunting. Briana mentions turkeys, grouse, deer, and elk, while Taziana relates to the hunt of a mountain lion.

Children in these communities learn to speak of hunting practices from different perspectives. They often address the danger or difficulty of hunting an animal in its own environment. They will also speak of the necessity of the hunt, for procuring meat, for protecting livestock and pets, for adventuring the wilderness, and for guiding outsiders (these are often humorous stories based on the incompetence of nonmountain folk to care for themselves or to understand the environment). Similarly children learn to speak of their respect for wildlife and a general reverence for life. Hunting is a means to an end; rarely is it valued solely for the thrill of a kill.

Another learned perspective regarding animals refers to a cultural understanding of animal taxonomy. Brianna uses the terms of *venaos y alasan*. Referring to an elk as an *alasan* distinguishes between elk and deer by reference to color differences. *Alasan* is a reddish-brown color. Deer are often referred to a *pardos* (gray colored). This indigenous distinction between different species of animals references a folk taxonomy that sees the animal species as similar in usefulness (food, hide), hunting practices, and relationship with humans. Where the animal species are dissimilar is reduced to simple color differences.

Another strategy for narrative and for conversation refers to an understanding of land stewardship. Children often reiterate adults' orientations to the value of maintaining effective conservation strategies as well as speaking with reverence about the beauty and sacredness of the natural environment. This way of speaking praises the natural environment and also honors human-created ecosystems such as the *acequia* and mountain trails. It is not uncommon to hear children speak of the *acequia* system as being similar to the human circulatory system. This is not a coincidence, since many of the Spanish words for *acequia* components are the same words as used for the circulatory system.

Children learn to recognize the importance of speaking with these and other strategies not only from the structuring of their speech but also from reading the contexts that call for such language strategies. They come to recognize when particular narratives are appreciated and when it is appropriate to elaborate. Not all discussions have the purpose of elucidating villager conceptualizations of place, environment, and community. They are context specific constructions that are more common at informal settings and familiar events. To the degree that children (and educators) become more familiar with content and context for place-based discussions, the more support will be provided to a structured transmission of cultural knowledge and community cohesion.

Analysis of local narratives has demonstrated a great potential to determine concepts of significance for children and adults. To the degree that we determine common narrative elements and identifiable patterns, we will be able to recognize important information for the community and families. Narrative accounts of events, shared stories, and personal experiences provide us with additional insight into meaningful phenomena idiosyncratic to the region.

Place, Story, and Schooling

Mas que el regalo, se estima la manera de darlo (More meaningful than the gift is the manner in which it is given)

Research into story, narrative, and general conversation provides us with meaningful insights into the essence of a culture or community. One does not need to look far, for these utterances are much a part of our daily lives. They are scattered through a variety of vernacular contexts and relationships in homes, stores, bus rides, and many other areas. The research activity may be a simple methodology of listening intently and sincerely. By listening with a genuine interest we can actually "sponsor" the salvage and continuance of narratives that can bring us so much perspective into divergent people's lives. The "sponsorship" of story thus becomes an exercise in democracy supporting divergent ideas and realities.

When exercised in institutional contexts, it can become an "empowerment" activity that can help reform institutional practices that have not been able to "hear" the relevance and urgency for community voices that are different from hegemonic cultural practices. Schools, above other social institutions, hold a grand potential for this progressive endeavor. School systems have historically stifled the type of story that is most expressive of cultural values. Perhaps it is a time for substantive reform that not only questions the canonical "gift" of the institution but also questions the manner in which advancement is achieved. Place-based story can serve as a medium by which students can become more active members of the process that has the most power to impact their lives and communities. Schooling that presents a concern for multicultural empowerment must recognize different strategies and arenas by which it can include cultural groups that have a version of success that is not necessarily reflected in generic teaching materials. Perhaps an ongoing exploration into place and story can increase the partnerships that most benefit learning and development.

Notes

1. The terms "Chicano," "Mexican American," and "Hispanic" are used interchangeably throughout this chapter. However, the term *manito* specifically refers to rural Chicanos from northern New Mexico and southern Colorado.

2. The study takes place in the area of Sapello, a small mountain community about seventy miles east of Santa Fe. Student interviews were conducted with students from many smaller communities surrounding the school of Sapello.

References

Arellano, Juan Estevan. 1997."La Querencia: La Raza Bioregionalism." *New Mexico Historical Review* 72, no. 1: 31–37.

Arizpe, Lourdes. 1992. "Ethnicity, Nations, and Culture." *Development* 4: 6–8.

Atencio, Ernest. 2001. *Of Land and Culture: Environmental Justice and Public Lands Ranching in Northern New Mexico*. El Paso, TX: Quivara Coalition.

Basso, Keith. 1996. *Wisdom Sits in Places: Landscape and Language among the Western Apache*. Albuquerque: University of New Mexico Press.

Basso, Keith, and Steven Feld, eds. 1996. *Senses of Place*. Santa Fe, NM: School of American Research Press.

Briggs, Charles L. 1988. *Competence and Performance: The Creativity of Tradition in Mexicano Verbal Art*. Philadelphia: University of Pennsylvania Press.

deBuys, William. 1985. *Enchantment and Exploitation: The Life and Hard Times of a New Mexico Mountain Range*. Albuquerque: University of New Mexico Press.

Forrest, Suzanne. 1989. *The Preservation of the Village: New Mexico's Hispanics and the New Deal*. Albuquerque: University of New Mexico Press.

Foucault, Michel. 1980. *Power/Knowledge: Selected Interviews and Writings, 1972–1977*. New York: Pantheon.

Gifford, Robert. 1987. *Environmental Psychology: Principles and Practices*. Boston: Allyn & Bacon.

Gonzales, Norma. 2001. *I Am My Language: Discourses of Women and Children in the Borderlands*. Tucson: University of Arizona Press.

Harvey, David Justice. 1996. *Nature and the Geography of Difference*. Malden, MA: Blackwell.

Hirsch, Eric, and Michael O'Hanlon, eds. 1995. *The Anthropology of Landscape: Perspectives on Place and Space*. Oxford: Clarendon.

Hymes, Dell. 1996. *Ethnography, Linguistics, Narrative Inequality: Towards an Understanding of Voice*. Bristol, PA: Taylor & Francis.

Johnstone, Barbara. 1990. *Stories, Community, and Place: Narratives from Middle America*. Indianapolis: Indiana University Press.

Keefe, Susan Emily. 1992. "Ethnic Identity: The Domain of Perceptions of and Attachment to Ethnic Groups and Cultures." *Human Organization* 51, no. 1: 35–43.

Melville, Margarita B. 1983. "Ethnicity: An Analysis of Its Dynamism and Variability Focusing on the Mexican/Mexican American Interface." *American Ethnologist* 10, no. 2: 272–89.

Ochs, Elinor. 1993. *Culture and Language Development: Language Acquisition and Language Socialization in a Samoan Village*. New York: Cambridge University Press.

Ochs, Elinor, and Bambi B. Schieffelin, eds. 1993. *Language Socialization across Cultures*. New York: Cambridge University Press.

Pena, Devon G. 1998. "Los Animalitos: Culture, Ecology, and the Politics of Place in the Upper Rio Grande." In *Chicano Culture, Ecology, Politics: Subversive Kin*, ed. Devon G. Pena, 25–57. Tucson: University of Arizona Press.

Pulido, Laura. 1998. "Ecological Legitimacy and Cultural Essentialism: Hispano Grazing in Northern New Mexico." In *Chicano Culture, Ecology, Politics: Subversive Kin,* ed. Devon G. Pena, 121–40. Tucson: University of Arizona Press.

Rivera, Jose A. 1998. *Acequia Culture: Water, Land, and Community in the Southwest.* Albuquerque: University of New Mexico Press.

Rodman, Margaret C. 1992. "Empowering Place: Multilocality and Multivocality." *American Anthropologist* 94, no. 3: 640–56.

Rodriguez, Sylvia. 1987. "Land Water and Ethnic Identity in Taos." In *Land, Water, and Culture: New Perspectives on Hispanic Land Grants* ed. Charles L. Briggs and John R. Van Ness, 331–403. Albuquerque: University of New Mexico Press.

Swadesh, Frances Leon. 1974. *Los Primeros Pobladores: Hispanic Americans on the Ute Frontier.* Notre Dame, IN: University of Notre Dame Press.

Toolan, Michael. 1997. *Narrative: A Critical Linguistic Introduction.* New York: Routledge.

Van Ness, John R. 1987. "Hispanic Land Grants: Ecology and Subsistence in the Uplands of Northern New Mexico and Southern Colorado." In *Land, Water, and Culture: New Perspectives on Hispanic Land Grants* ed. Charles L. Briggs and John R. Van Ness, 141–214. Albuquerque: University of New Mexico Press.

Velez-Ibanez, Carlos G. 1997. *Border Visions: Mexican Cultures of the Southwest United States.* Tucson: University of Arizona Press.

Warren, Nancy Hunter. 1987. *Villages of Hispanic New Mexico.* Santa Fe, NM: School of American Research Press.

Zedeno, Maria Nieves. 2000. "On What People Make of Places." In *Social Theory in Archeology,* ed. M. B. Schiffer, 97–111. Salt Lake City: University of Utah Press.

APPENDIX 3.1
English Translation of Briana's Story

Briana's story (in translation) is presented as written with her utilization of punctuation and spelling.

I live in a beautiful valley. In the valley where I live, there is my house way back in the forest. On the ranch I have two cats. Their names are Skipper and Stinker. I also have three dogs. Their names are Boots, Spots, and Rosa. They are very good dogs. On my ranch we have deer and elk. We hunt them for food. We sometimes make jerky, which is very good. We also hunt turkey and grouse. In my valley there also live bears and coyotes. We have to be especially careful with the bears that are hungry. The coyotes are afraid of us and usually run away. The birds in my valley are big and small and very pretty. They chirp very beautiful. In my valley, I have to work very hard. On my ranch we brand cows, ride horses, and gather all the cattle. We use one cow for milk. My horse is named Whiskey. The others are Mayo, the buckskin, and the Appaloosa is named Wapo. How pretty are my horses. My father and uncle tame horses for roping and herding cattle and also to go riding. The trees and all the plants and flowers n my valley are pretty and beautiful. They smell so good. The river that runs in my valley is very nice. In the river you can see fish. Sometimes I fish with my dad and uncle. In the afternoon we have a fish fry for all my family. The church in my valley is small and pretty. It is the Church of St. Joseph. My parents got married in this little church in my valley. It is the church where I pray to Jesus, thank Jesus, and also confess to Jesus. My school is small and it's in Sapello, which is also part of my valley. I have many friends that go with me to school. Some old houses are still standing that were built by a lot of our grandparents. They were built with adobe and beams. Some people have restored some of these old houses. In the night my valley is also very beautiful. My family and I sometimes sit on the porch to look at the moon and stars. Oh how pretty and beautiful is my valley. The end.

4

Teacher Narratives of *Movimiento* Ideology and Bilingual Education

Armando L. Trujillo

O N DECEMBER 9, 1969, CHICANO STUDENTS IN CRYSTAL CITY, TEXAS, staged a three-week walkout of the public schools in protest against the discriminatory policies practiced by the Anglo school staff and administration (Shockley 1974; Hardgrave and Hinojosa 1975; Gutiérrez 1976).[1] The students, with the support of their parents and the Mexican American Youth Organization, presented the third of a series of petitions to the school board calling for relevant and equal quality education. The focus on relevant and equal education is reflected in the key demands calling for bilingual/bicultural education, the creation of a Mexican American history course for credit, and the recognition of *diez y seis de septiembre* (September 16) as a Mexican American holiday.[2] The local struggle for relevant, equal, quality education had been a long one, and was brought to regional and national attention by the massive student walkout. While the walkout strategy was successful and the students and parents won some initial concessions from the Anglo administration, the walkout achieved only modest change in the structure of ethnic power relations in the schooling domain (Smith and Foley 1975). It nonetheless constituted a moral victory for the Chicano community, for it was a statement of revitalized ethnic identity and gave the confrontation historical significance (Smith and Foley 1975). More than anything, this moral victory signaled the end of the era of local Anglo domination and ultimately led to Chicano control over schooling (Langenegger 1993; Trujillo 1998).

The Mexican American Youth Organization (MAYO) led by a Chicano activist-intellectual, José Angel Gutiérrez, helped students and parents in their struggle for relevant, equal educational opportunity and treatment (Navarro

1995; Gutiérrez 1998). Community support from the school walkout enabled MAYO to organize an alternative political party, Raza Unida, which became the vehicle for Chicano political mobilization and reform that eventually overturned the political and hegemonic domination imposed by the Anglo minority since the turn of the century.[3] The first step in this process took place in the local elections of 1970, where the Chicano community gained political control of both the school board and city council. After this important political victory, Crystal City and the Raza Unida Party (RUP) became a major icon for the Chicano civil rights movement in Texas and throughout the Southwest (Navarro 1998).[4]

After gaining political control in Crystal City, the RUP initiated a variety of reform programs designed to empower the Chicano community; among them was a mixture of housing, mental health, health care, economic development, and education programs. Of the different reform programs, those that focused on improving education became prominent. Schools are a pivotal institution in any community, for they are instrumental in processes of socialization and the transmission of knowledge. In Crystal City, where the future direction of a political movement was based on the tenet of self-determination, the control of governing institutions including schools was imperative (Gutiérrez 1976). José Angel Gutiérrez, the school board president of the Crystal City School District from 1970 to 1972 and founder of the RUP in Zavala County, expresses his view (and by extension the RUP view) of education in an interview in a documentary film in the early 1970s:

> Education in this kind of society is mandatory if not a prerequisite for survival. [It] is also the fountain of socialization where our values get distorted and cultural imposition takes place. Not only do we want to reject that, but also we want to substitute that with our own values, which are just as dear and important. Education, finally, is important for us because from that kind of leadership that will emerge from those schools we will have the leaders for tomorrow, to build a greater *Aztlán.* (Reskin and Williams 1974)

Gutiérrez's statement captures the emergent cultural nationalist philosophy of the RUP in the early 1970s. Moreover, it reflects the ideological position of the role that schools were expected to play with respect to socialization and the maintenance of the language and culture. My use of the term "ideology" is analogous to how Barker and Galasinski (2001) use the concept—it refers to the general and social representations shared by members of a group and used by them to accomplish everyday social practices. They add that "these representations are organized into systems which are deployed by social classes and other groups in order to make sense of, figure out and render intelligible the way the society works" (Barker and Galasinski 2001, 66). In this manner, ideology serves as a mechanism for both communication and action. Yet this conception also implies that it is an area where struggle takes place.

The narrative statement by Gutiérrez identifies key areas of ideological struggle that developed after the RUP takeover. In particular, struggles ensued over the language of instruction, cultural values represented in the schooling domain, and socialization. Gutiérrez makes it clear that the type of education that Chicano students had received under Anglo-controlled schooling was one of cultural imposition. The student petitions presented to the school board in 1969 articulated a reaction against these impositions. One of the areas that Chicanos in Cristal[5] and elsewhere in the broader Chicano movement struggled to change was the language of instruction, which was exclusively in English. Consequently, students and parents called for the implementation of bilingual education. Another area of contention addressed by the petitions was the absence within the school curriculum of the contributions made by Mexican Americans to the history and culture of Texas and the United States. As a result, students called for the creation of a Chicano history course and the recognition of Mexican Independence day *(diez y seis de septiembre)* as a school holiday, which would publicly validate the cultural history of the Mexican community. These examples illustrate areas of ideological struggle that were set in motion in the early 1970s.

The schools became the site and the target of a concentrated effort to construct different forms of knowledge and identities, which countered those produced during the era of Anglo-controlled schooling. The changes in the structure of schooling in Crystal City initiated under the RUP were part of a larger political vision where the discourse of nationalism, self-determination, and *Aztlán* were central. I refer to the vision and the action taken by Chicano educators to put this plan into practice as the cultural production of a Chicano/Chicana "educated person." Central to this vision was the implementation of a comprehensive K-12 bilingual/bicultural education program through which educators would provide relevant, equal education. However, the schooling project initiated by Chicano leaders and educators in the early 1970s was initially embraced and later resisted by teachers and parents. It is therefore necessary to analyze the extent to which Chicano educators shared the general and social representations of the larger political vision of *el movimiento*, the RUP, and bicultural/bilingual schooling. In this chapter, I discuss the nature of these social/ideological representations by drawing on the narratives of Chicano teachers (many of them were students during the walkout) and their retrospective look at *el movimiento*, the RUP, and bicultural/bilingual education.

Theoretical Framework

The concept of cultural *production* is akin to the notion of "emergent culture" as used by Raymond Williams (1973). Bauman refers to emergent culture as that process of continuous creation of new meanings and values, new practices, new significances and experiences (1977, 48). In studies of education the concept of cultural production has been used to portray the way people actively confront the ideological and material conditions presented by schooling (Levinson and Holland 1996). The RUP's philosophy of cultural nationalism, when channeled through the institution of schooling, was tantamount to the cultural production of an emergent Chicano/Chicana "educated person." When placed within the historical context and discourse of *Aztlán* and cultural nationalism, education leaders in Crystal City were striving to create bilingual and bicultural Chicanos and Chicanas who would not only be able to survive in the mainstream society, but more than that, they were hoping to create the future leaders who would carry forth the struggle of building a greater *Aztlán* (Gutiérrez 1976, 1998).

Through a comprehensive philosophy of bilingual/bicultural education, Chicano leaders in the school district sought to reverse the effects of acculturative and assimilative schooling under Anglo control and cultivate a "new" Chicano worldview (Smith and Foley 1978). In other words, they sought to create a "subject-position" (Levinson and Holland 1996) for a Chicano/ Chicana "educated person," specifically a bilingual, culturally proud, community-oriented individual. In keeping with the vision espoused by José Angel Gutiérrez, leaders sought to create politicized subjects in line with the distinct cultural and political-economic interests of the RUP. The degree to which the RUP achieved this goal remains an area of contention. Further discussion of this debate is found later in this chapter following an examination of the narrative evidence provided by teachers.

When one looks at the relationship between *el movimiento* and the RUP in restructuring schooling opportunities for Chicano students, one finds few recent studies that have looked at this question directly. A few studies were done in the 1970s that looked at the relationship between political mobilization and schooling change during the height of the *movimiento* (Post 1975; Smith and Foley 1975, 1978; Smith 1978). Foley (1990) did a follow-up ethnographic study in a community not too far from Cristal, where the RUP was very active in the 1970s. He focuses on the high school and how schooling practices changed in response to the Chicano civil rights movement. He found that while there is a relationship between political process and schooling— the ethnic makeup of the student, teacher, and administrative composition of the schools changed to reflect the ethnic makeup of the Chicano majority in the community—the overall function of schooling remained intact. That is, the schools continue to reproduce class inequalities along ethnic lines. Foley's study sheds light on the limitations of ethnic political mobilization in changing the fundamental role that schools play in society. Moreover, his study reveals how classroom practices as mediated through language help reproduce inequality. Foley's research did not look at the relationship between Chicano nationalism, identity, and bilingual/bicultural education. However, his focus on language is crucial, for language is central to discovering the shared meanings of culture. Barker and Galasinski state that "to understand culture is to explore how meaning is produced symbolically through the signifying practices of language within material and institutional contexts" (2001, 4). Given my overall goal—to discover the meaning that *movimiento* ideology has for Chicano educators—it is necessary to look at narrative as a way of understanding the impact that the *movimiento* and the RUP had in the lives of Chicanos in Cristal.

The Use of Narrative Analysis

Teacher narratives have the advantage of placing teachers centrally within the analysis and evaluation of the educational reforms introduced under the RUP. In this manner, teachers serve the role of social critic. According to Walzer, "social criticism involves making complex ethical judgments about existing social arrangements" (cited in Rosaldo 1993, 182). Rosaldo adds that such moral vision emerges from within the society under criticism and not from the outside (1993, 182). From this perspective, the voices that emerge from teacher narratives serve as a reflexive evaluation of why things changed in Cristal following the post-RUP days. "Social critics," says Rosaldo, "work outward from in-depth knowledge of a specific form of life . . . rather than downward from abstract principles" (194). The narratives that I collected from teachers present an emic (or insider) view of what is meaningful to the social actors in the setting, or how meaning is constructed over time. With respect to the ethnographic representation of meaning, Barker and Galasinski note that using a more dialogical approach to research ensures that "ethnography becomes less an expedition in search of 'the facts' and more a conversation between participants in an investigative process" (2001, 9).

Further advantages to the use of narrative analysis emerge when one looks at the relationship between narrative and "historical understanding," and questions of "human agency." Rosaldo refers to the former as "the interaction of ideas, events and institutions as they change through time"; the latter "designates the study of the feelings and intentions of social actors"

(1993, 127). My use of teacher narratives has the advantage of providing a historical understanding of the ideas that were initiated with the *movimiento* as well as how these ideas affected the institution of schooling and bilingual education through time (another function of narrative is to capture a sense of time). A focus on human agency and narrative analysis, on the other hand, provides insight into the feelings and intentions of Chicano/Chicana educators as they sought to implement the ideas of *el movimiento* into educational practice.

In this chapter, I pursue this line of analysis by looking at the narratives of Chicano educators (many of them were students during the walkout) and their retrospective look at *el movimiento*, the RUP, and bilingual/bicultural education.

Methods and Data Sources

In this section I use a historical and ethnographic framework to study the relationship between political ideology, ethnic identity, teaching philosophy, and bilingual schooling. While I focus on the educational reforms introduced under the RUP, I do not restrict my research solely to the school site, however. Following Levinson and Holland (1996), I regard the school as a symbolic social space that generates different kinds of social relations of dominance or resistance. Working from this premise, I focus on the interrelation between Chicano community political process, identity formation, and bilingual/bicultural education, and have collected data from individuals at the school and community level. To analyze the educational practices and discourses linking these different levels, I utilize a multilevel ethnographic approach. Ogbu (1981) argues that multilevel ethnography uses both transactional and structural questions to explore the linkages between schooling and the larger sociocultural system. By focusing on multiple levels of interaction, I demonstrate that politics, identity, and teaching philosophy are produced through the interaction of multiple discourses and voices.

I use a combination of qualitative methods and traditions (Erickson 1986; Bogdan and Biklen 1982) stemming from approximately sixteen months of ethnographic fieldwork in the community. The methods and traditions include participant observation, unstructured interviews, questionnaires, and the collection of school documents. Primary data sources for this chapter consist of interviews with classroom teachers. Most of the teachers I interviewed had taught in the bilingual program in the 1970s or early 1980s before the bilingual program was restructured. The majority of the interviews were tape-recorded and later transcribed. In a few instances, however, teachers did not want the interview tape-recorded. Then I took notes of the interview in my fieldwork notebook. Once the interviews were transcribed, I read the interviews and did initial open coding to generate a list of topics (Emerson, Fretz, and Shaw 1996). From this initial long list, I grouped related topics into emergent categories that corresponded to my overall focus on *movimiento* ideology and bilingual education. In subsequent steps, I created files from the pertinent coded categories from the teacher interviews, which I read and coded, for a further refinement of topics. I followed this step by writing initial memos to deepen the analysis in accordance to the procedures discussed in Emerson, Fretz, and Shaw (1996). Initial coding and memo writing yielded numerous themes. In this chapter, however, I confine my analysis and discussion to themes that give insight into *movimiento* ideology, identity, and bilingual/bicultural education. I also follow a critical discourse framework (Barker and Galasinski 2001; Fairclough 1995) in analyzing pertinent narrative samples from the teacher interviews. Before proceeding to a discussion of the central themes, I want to stress that the Chicano teachers I interacted with during the time I collected data were most cooperative in sharing their time and information with me. I believe that their narratives are key links and depositories of information given that they experienced the changes that the community and schools have undergone since 1969. In this respect, they meet the criteria of the social critic. As Rosaldo has noted, social actors who have experienced that which they are commenting on "work outward from in-depth knowledge of a specific form of life" (1993, 194). Using the information that teachers shared with me, I have pieced together an emic story of change and persistence within the broader sociopolitical and economic context of South Texas.

Central Themes and Narrative Excerpts from Teachers

Interviews were conducted with teachers at four schools—elementary school, middle school, junior high, and high school. The following prominent themes emerged after coding and analysis of the interviews with teachers. I provide a composite summary of the theme based on what teachers said. Following this characterization, I include narrative excerpts that illustrate the theme and provide insight into the two aspects of narrative analysis that Rosaldo (1993) underscored: historical understanding and human agency. The focus on human agency provides further insight into the feelings and intentions of Chicana/Chicano educators as they were shaped and influenced by the ideas of *el movimiento* and educational practice.

El Movimiento and the Raza Unida Party

The Chicano civil rights movement provides the broader political-historical context for situating the narratives of Chicano educators. One of the early documents that represent this ideological discourse among Chicano leaders is found in *El Plan de Aztlán* (Camejo 1971; http://latino.sscnet.ucla.edu/research/docs/struggle/aztlan.htm).[6] This document captures in text the theme of nationalism as the central key for mobilization and organization leading to self-determination. The text further delineates seven organizational goals and six steps for action, of which establishing an independent political party was paramount. Among the prominent goals identified in the plan and articulated by Chicano leaders were unity, economic control of communities and institutions, relevant education, including bilingual education, cultural values that strengthen family, home, and group identity (e.g., *carnalismo* or brotherhood), and political liberation. An empirical example of how these goals were put into action is found in Gutiérrez's autobiographical book. It provides an insider's elaboration of cultural nationalism and community organizing (e.g., the role of MAYO in the school walkout and the subsequent evolution of the RUP in Cristal and Zavala County [Gutiérrez 1998]). Both *El Plan de Aztlán* and the treatise by Gutiérrez provide a textual starting point for exploring the extent to which Chicano educators shared the general and social representations of Chicano nationalist ideology.

In Crystal City, following the RUP electoral victories in the school board and city council elections, Chicano leaders developed programs that would further the goals outlined in *El Plan*. The statement made by José Angel Gutiérrez (see above) emphasizes the role of education in promoting cultural values and the overall goal of self-determination. One of my primary research concerns was to look at the relationship between *movimiento* leaders' ideological discourse and corresponding changes in people's aspirations and behaviors. Therefore, in my conversations with Chicano educators I asked them to comment on the *movimiento* and its impact. With few exceptions, the vast majority of them stated that the *movimiento* had brought positive change. Those who voiced a different opinion noted that it had been harmful. Regardless of whether the *movimiento* was perceived as good or harmful, all agreed that it changed the previous education structure, which had been controlled by the Anglo minority. Teachers also recalled that the *movimiento* had not only served as a catalyst for cultural awareness and pride but also helped raise the educational aspirations of Mexican Americans in Crystal City. For example, Sara Lujan, a teacher who had been one of the primary student leaders during the walkout, reflected on the meaning *el movimiento* and the RUP:

For me, it made me know who I was, appreciate my roots and be proud of them. It gave me the confidence that yes I could go to college, that it was possible, and I could pursue higher aspirations than a secretary. I think more than anything else it gave . . . I'm not going to speak for everybody . . . but it gave me pride in who I was and the confidence that I could do anything I wanted to do in life, which I didn't have before. Now [post walkout], I no longer felt less than somebody that was totally English speaking or Anglo . . . the way they use to make us feel. I no longer felt that way. I'd walk into that, ah, drug store and feel just as proud to be in there and just as sure of myself, which I never did have before the *movimiento*. For me it was something good.

Barker and Galasinski state that "ethnicity is a relational concept concerned with categories of self-identification and social ascription" (2001, 123). That is, ethnic identity involves a comparison with the other and is constituted through power relations between groups (Melville 1983; Barker and Galasinski 2001). Barth (1969) refers to ethnicity as a process of boundary formation that is constructed and maintained under specific sociohistorical conditions. In Cristal the comparison is with the Anglo-American, which prior to the Chicano takeover in 1972 had been the dominant other. The discourse that Sara Lujan employs in reference to her identity alludes to the historical and cultural legacy of Chicanos as well as to overcoming relations of marginality and subordination. This insight points to questions of agency or the study of the feelings and intentions of social actors (Rosaldo 1993). The teachers I talked with often stated that as students they felt subordinate to or less confident in the presence of the Anglo other. However, through the ideas associated with the discourse of the *movimiento* (e.g., *Aztlán*, self-determination, and *Chicanismo*) Chicanas and Chicanos in Cristal gained a new confidence in their culture and their capacity to achieve higher levels of education and the rewards that come with this.

Marcos Manriquez, a third grade teacher who was a freshman in high school during the walkout, provides another example. During our interview, Manriquez characterized himself as not being politically aware of all the issues at the time: "I wasn't aware of what was going on . . . all of a sudden I just knew that all these kids had walked out . . . I didn't know what was going on, I was still sitting in the classroom, and here's all my friends and buddies walking outside . . . You know, calling me a turncoat—brown on the outside and white on the inside." He adds that the walkout event caused him to quickly educate himself by talking to his more knowledgeable classmates who informed him of the issues. As a result, he decided to act:

. . . so after the following period, I went outside and checked and they said here's the situation, there's a walkout because of what happened to the cheerleaders and all this and I think that was just the straw that broke the camel's back. You know that's what started everything . . . there were things that always occurred where the Mexican American was being discriminated . . . After . . . I found out a few odds and ends, at that time, like I said, I wasn't really gung-ho. I was a kid. I was about fifteen years old, and I said, what the heck, I'm going to walk out too. But after a while, you know, I realized what was going on and this and that and in my own mind I just said well I'm just gonna, I'm just . . . going to go with the flow. I'm just going to go with the majority rule. If the people decide that this is better for the people, I'm going to go with that. If they think that we should walk out for the rest of the year, then I'm going to go with that. So we just stayed out. I don't recall how long it was.

Manriquez illustrates the multidimensionality of how agency operates in "the role of the human actor as individual or group in directing or effectively intervening in the course of history" (Brooker 1999, 3). Awareness of the group's concerns enabled him "to go with the flow" and in the process gain critical consciousness of both his ethnicity and the concerns of the group. Participating in the group political process enabled him to gain a higher level of political awareness with respect to his identity. This is reflected in his response to my question on how the Chicano *movimiento* experience affected him and his community:

What it did to me is it made me more aware of who I was as a . . . my ethnic background. You know, I did start thinking more about, well, our people need to, you know, wishing and hoping that our people in general would become better educated. So that they could, so that it would give them more choices in life. More than anything else, I wanted, I hated to see, you know, all these Mexican Americans not having the ability to make their own choices . . . And to a certain extent, I believe that the movement, yes, was good in the sense of political awareness, bringing the people to grip with themselves about their ethnicity, their culture, their race and everything, which is fantastic, but on the flip side of that, it also brought out the worst in some people.

Javier Velez, a third grade teacher who was in the junior high at the time of the walkout, provides a slightly different experience:

I was in seventh grade during the walkout. I still believe that I was, if not the first one, maybe in the first four or five to walk out of the junior high at the time . . . When I went home I told my mom what was going on and she said that she knew about it and for me to stay out and join the line and enter the walkout so I did. We went all over the place. We walked through all the different schools.

After the walkout and during the time that the RUP controlled the governing institutions in the community, he participated in various community activities. For example, he recalls getting involved in the election campaigns of the Raza Unida Party by helping to get the vote out:

> I started my involvement in community activities . . . I would volunteer to go with a whole bunch of other kids to . . . like when it came to voting time on election day we'd go and walk the streets with little cards, index cards, and each one had the number of a family and their address and how many members in the family that were voting age. We'd go and they'd assign us a street with the little cards and we'd go knocking on those particular doors only, and we would ask if those people lived there and if so if they had gone to vote . . . I did that in eighth grade and all through high school.

With respect to postsecondary education, Javier Velez credits his parents and siblings with much of the motivation for going to college. However, he also acknowledges his community involvement during the *movimiento* as reinforcing his long-term commitment to education and his community. I asked him how central education was to the *movimiento*:

> Oh yes, that was one of the major goals. Everybody, the way I heard it then . . . maybe it was the way I perceived it, okay, because you know how tricky words can be sometimes . . . We want everybody to go to college. It's the only way you're going to succeed in this world and the world to come, you know, and the . . . future. I worked for 100 percent besides getting that from my parents okay. That's why I decided to go to college, educate myself and come back to Cristal to further that goal. Get kids, you know, really motivated to go to college, not just finish high school, but think about finishing college. That's why I came back.

The narrative excerpts of the teachers discussed above illustrate the relationship between the ideas articulated in the ideological discourse of cultural nationalism, in particular ethnic identity, postsecondary education, and commitment to serve la Raza. The voices that emerge from the teacher narratives reveal the positive link between the broader *movimiento* and changes at the local level. Specifically the narratives shed light on how and why teachers gained greater awareness of their ethnicity, which in turn motivated them to pursue a university education and the long-term commitment to serve their community. The narrative excerpts also show the complexity of ethnicity and its dynamic quality. Barker and Galasinski observe, "Ethnicity is not a static entity based on primordial ties or universal cultural characteristics possessed by a specific group for identities are unpredictable productions of a specific history and culture" (2001, 123). The narrative excerpts discussed above reveal that the production of ethnic identity and the action taken by Chicano educators at the particular historical moment and subsequently is, as Barker and Galasinski (2001) note, an evolving "discursive construction." In this respect, teachers talk about their identity in relation to not only the Anglo other but also the larger organizational context of the nation-state. Teachers were cognizant of the fact that historically Mexican Americans were marginalized as second-class citizens. They understood that the *movimiento* was a political struggle for greater inclusion within the nation-state system. Thus it was not uncommon for teachers to discuss their cultural distinctiveness (ethnicity) by referring to their national identity. Javier Velez illustrates this point in his response to me asking what the *movimiento* meant for him:

> Bottom line. That I didn't have to take shit just because I'm a Chicano, that I'm an American. Somebody asked me, what are you? I'm American, okay. What's your ethnic background? They would ask me that. Chicano, okay, but I'm an American first. I didn't have to stand for people telling me you're not an American, you're Mexican, and you're not a first-class citizen, you're a second-class citizen. I had to put up with that stuff. Not only did I [not] have to put up with it but also I was given ammunition to be able to defend myself to say why I don't have to put up with that shit. That puts it bluntly.

Hall notes that the concept of ethnicity "acknowledges the place of history, language, and culture in the construction of subjectivity and identity" (1996, 446). One must keep in mind, however, that the discourse on ethnicity takes place in a particular historical, social, and political context, which means that ethnicity changes over time. With respect to Chicano ethnicity, the discourse of cultural nationalism, *Aztlán*, and self-determination presented one vision of what it meant to be a Chicano in the early 1970s. In Crystal City the RUP took steps to implement this vision in the schools through bilingual/bicultural education. However, as the following discussion shows, the bilingual education program came under pressure from various fronts to change its emphasis on cultural distinctiveness and Spanish-language instruction to one that gave primacy to English-language instruction and mainstream curriculum.

Bilingual/Bicultural Education and *Movimiento* Politics

In the early 1970s, the school board adopted a policy detailing twenty-two recommendations for changing the curricular program in the district.[7] In spirit and content these recommendations incorporated the key demands put forth in the student petition in 1969, including bilingual/bicultural education, the inclusion of Chicano culture in the curriculum, and the recognition of *diez y seis de septiembre* as a Mexican American holiday. The central cog of this policy document, however, was a comprehensive bilingual/bicultural program spanning all twelve grades. The overall goal was to graduate bilingual, biliterate, and bicultural students. Spanish and English were given equal standing as languages of instruction and Chicano/Mexican culture was emphasized in curriculum content and activities. During the height of the *movimiento* the program generated interest as it validated the language and culture of Mexican Americans. Moreover, it was seen as an innovative program designed to provide relevant educational opportunities for students to learn content in their native language and in the process acquire English. Bilingual education was a new experimental program in the early 1970s (Padilla 1984), but since it came in with the politics of the movement it was mired in politics. The history of this program in Cristal from the 1970s to the 1990s is one of change in goals, structure, and content. The following teacher excerpts highlight some of these changes in its implementation and development. As such, these narratives function as a reflexive evaluation of why the program changed.

One of the early challenges facing RUP education leaders when they took control of the school district was a shortage of qualified bilingual teachers. The goal of developing and implementing a comprehensive K-12 bilingual/bicultural program, as outlined in the twenty-two recommendations, challenged district leaders to fill teaching positions with qualified bilingual teachers at all levels. The bilingual teacher shortage was compounded because many of the old-guard teachers were replaced when the RUP took control. The new replacements were mostly teachers with no experience in bilingual education. One strategy that district leaders used to meet the need for bilingual teachers was to recruit and train paraprofessionals from the district. The Career Opportunity Program (COP) was a federally funded program that enabled teacher aides to obtain their bachelor's degree and certification by attending university classes at night, on weekends, and full-time during the summer. The program was brought in by RUP leaders in the school district. While this program provided opportunities for Chicanas and Chicanos to obtain their university training and credentials, it also created tension in the teaching ranks. Elida Salinas became a bilingual teacher and a COP participant during the 1970s:

> I would say that the regular staff that had been here for a long time were a little upset because they hired us . . . I think they saw us like we were community people and not necessarily people who should be working in the schools. That's how I felt. I remember the principal called a meeting . . . well, it was his orders . . . one of the teachers, Mexican American teacher had a meeting with us and she told us, you girls better start dressing up . . . I guess maybe we weren't dressed up; it takes time to become a professional . . . I felt like they really didn't want us there. I mean, I could see it in the eyes of not only the Anglo teachers, but the Mexican American teachers that had been there a long time.

In spite of the internal animosity and discomfort that it brought into the school setting, the COP program was seen overall as a successful program. It afforded opportunities for working-class Chicanas and Chicanos to obtain their university training and participate in the process of social assimilation through economic mobility. Salinas was not the only one to benefit from the program:

> Some of the principals, the principal at the junior high and the principal at the high school . . . were aides. Have you talked to Ms. N? She was a teacher's aide. Ms. M. was a teacher aide. They were all teacher aides. Mr. T. up there at— elementary, he is teaching second grade. It was just a lot of us who were aides. We became professionals and . . . we took the places of the teachers that left, because the Anglos left.

The challenge of finding qualified teachers became less problematic over time as more Mexican Americans obtained their university credentials and returned to the community to work. However, other challenges emerged that became more problematic in fulfilling the goal of maintaining a viable K-12 bilingual/bicultural education program. I have elsewhere analyzed the confluence of factors and forces that eventually led to the restructuring of the bilingual/bicultural education program (see Trujillo 1998). In this chapter I focus on teachers' recollections of the factors that contributed to change. Ironically, language of instruction and curriculum content surfaced as a concern.

Insight into the language of instruction and curriculum content is provided by Linda Nieves, a native of Cristal who graduated from high school in 1968; consequently, she missed out on the walkout by a year. She went to the university, obtained her bachelor's degree, and was hired as a bilingual teacher in the early 1970s. When I interviewed her, she was teaching in a nonbilingual second grade but had taught in the bilingual program from the 1970s to the mid-1980s. She recalls that the bilingual program in the 1970s emphasized using Spanish and incorporating Mexican culture.

> We'd say the Pledge of Allegiance in Spanish and we would do so a lot. There was a lot of material developed . . . I know as the years passed it began to diminish somewhat . . . We had a lot of . . . it. Our curriculum was rich in a lot of the . . . in both cultures, you know . . . For a while there was more of the Mexican culture . . . that was very predominant in our curriculum, and I remember we wouldn't tell the kids about Columbus Day. Then it sort of went lopsided for a while and then it sort of came back, and I don't know at this point if we still do it. I think it's more of on an even scale now because during that time, during the early '70s we were really, really emphasizing the Mexican culture a lot.

Henriqueta Toralva is a fourth grade language arts teacher who graduated from Crystal City High School, attended the university, obtained her bachelor's degree, and then returned to teach. She also recalls the focus of the program in the 1970s and alludes to one of the concerns that eventually led to programmatic change.

> The bilingual program was a good idea . . . in my opinion. I felt that it was good in a way *y en otra manera* it hurt our students. Maybe because the implementation of the program was not, it was not implemented the way it should have been. I think that's mainly the . . . concern. Because it was good *que* they were teaching our children, *y digo* our children because they are our students . . . they wanted our children to learn, you know, the Spanish language to learn about *la cultura de ellos* and all of this was fine. But it got to a point that they wanted two programs *que fueran* one-to-one, en *un nivel.* What happened was that a lot of our students could not handle *las dos idiomas* [both languages] at the same time. There was a time where *le estaban poninedo mas* emphasis *en el* Spanish [and] the English language was staying behind.

Toralva alludes to the tension that developed in the teaching ranks concerning language of instruction and curricular content. The broader context of this internal tension concerns the confluence of national, state, and local politics, which eventually led to the demise of the RUP and the restructuring of the K-12 bilingual/bicultural education program.

The Raza Unida Party in Crystal City ceased to be a viable party by the late 1970s. José Angel Gutiérrez was serving his second term as county judge at the time. However, he was forced to resign his post in 1981 by the more conservative county commissioners who disagreed with his politics and his high absenteeism (Gutiérrez 1998; Trujillo 1998). He eventually left Texas and relocated to Oregon. The county and the school district then entered a new period of politics that reflected the status quo and the conservative political sentiment at the national and state level. National and state educational policy affecting bilingual education composed the broader forces that impacted local level policy changes and practice (Trujillo 1998). Padilla (1984) notes that Title VII bilingual education program policy shifted from focusing on innovation and experimentation to transitional programs with a focus on English language instruction. These broader factors and forces had a profound impact on teachers and educational policy and practice at the district level.

In the early 1980s the program was restructured to serve students in kindergarten through fifth grade. The educators I interviewed often cited national and state education policy among the main factors contributing to the change. The unforeseen impact of removing bilingual instruction from grades seven through twelve had further repercussions during the 1984–1985 school year. The program was reorganized into a pre-kindergarten through first grade program. The aim of this reorganization was to transition limited English-speaking students into English-only classrooms by the end of the first grade, even if they had not fully mastered English. In a span of roughly twelve years the goal of the bilingual education program had changed completely. During the 1970s and early 1980s the goal was to use the native language and culture as a valuable resource and produce bilingual, biliterate, and bicultural students. By the mid-1980s the goal changed to the use of native language instruction as a transition into English-only instruction by the start of first grade. Teachers attribute the substantive restructuring of the bilingual education program to external and internal forces. In what follows I focus on the major internal forces affecting educational practice identified by teachers.

The most commonly cited internal force was standardized testing. Several teachers said that their students scored low on national and state-mandated tests such as the California Test of Basic Skills (CTBS) and Texas Educational Assessment of Minimal Skills (TEAMS).[8] The low scores caused alarm among teachers and parents and brought the focus on the bilingual/bicultural maintenance program, which was often cited as the reason for the low scores. Students in Cristal were at a disadvantage, since standardized tests are administered in English. Moreover, with national bilingual education policy emphasizing transitional bilingual education, many educators and parents began to attribute the low scores to a lack of English instruction.

Jessica Rimares, a fourth and fifth grade teacher who has taught in the bilingual program since 1980, expresses the concerns of teachers over low scores on standardize tests: "Our English scores in our achievement test were real low. And we needed to do something drastic at that point to bring them up . . . We felt that the students weren't getting enough practice as far as reading or conjugating or anything in English, not enough practice was occurring." Rimares was one of the teachers who agreed with the restructuring of the bilingual program into a K-1 transitional program. She attributes the impetus for change to low student scores on standardized tests:

> Now . . . thinking back as to why there was a big change as far as the comprehensive bilingual program here at our campus for the fourth and fifth grade level, that was the TABS (Texas Assessment of Basic Skills), back then it was TABS, it is a relative of TEAMS test now. I think that is why, you know because our students need a little bit more help as far as English was concerned. We were, I guess the district felt that they were forced . . . to make that change. And you know that you have to keep up with the TEAMS and you . . . have to keep up state norms or whatever.

She goes on to express her satisfaction with the changes in the structure and goals of the program, especially since it has improved student results on standardized test.

I feel pretty good about the system because the first year that I was here, I remember looking at our achievement scores and I think we had about, which sounds pretty bad, 19 percent mastering the CTBS, whatever our test was at the time. And we had just got our TEAMS test results Friday and the principals presented them to us . . . and we're up to something like 87 percent mastery. This is a big jump in the seven years that I have been here, so we're obviously doing something right.

While Rimares argues that something had to be done to improve the student test performance, she expressed some concern with the elimination of Spanish instruction from the curriculum: "I personally saw a need, maybe not necessarily to drop the Spanish, but there was a strong need for our students because they, the majority of the student population, I felt weren't fluent in Spanish or English. We had some that were very fluent in both, but I felt that there wasn't enough to justify. Personally, that's how I felt."

Henriqueta Toralva seconds Rimares's sentiments, noting that the concern for improving English language proficiency and testing outcomes came from teachers in the junior high and high school. The concern that was voiced by junior high teachers came after the bilingual program was reorganized into a K-fifth grade program. Teachers complained that students entering junior high school were not proficient English speakers. According to Toralva, students had a difficult time settling into the junior high instructional flow because they had not transitioned out of Spanish into English.

> . . . *todavia los tenian en* Spanish and . . . they would go on to junior high and half the students would be behind in the English language. They [the teachers] were seeing *en donde les estaba afectando,* in the junior high level and then into high school. That's when . . . a lot of concern was coming on *que* hey, what are you doing with those children *que nos estan mandando aca sin leer* [that you are sending without being able to read] and all this . . . a lot of pressure.

Parental input was one of the other forces, aside from test scores and English language proficiency, that teachers talked about as the impetus behind the restructuring of the bilingual/bicultural education program. Teachers report that parents often expressed anger that their children could not speak English well and were reading at low levels. They add that parents began to push for more English instruction because they wanted their children to improve their English reading and do better on standardized tests. Many of them reasoned that improved English skills would facilitate entry into the mainstream and make students more competitive once they left Crystal City. The change in the structure and focus of the bilingual program from maintenance to transitional resulted in changed goals and outcomes. In the 1970s the ultimate goal was to produce biliterate students in two languages. In the 1980s the goal was to use native language instruction as a bridge to English-only instruction. Students who qualified for the transitional bilingual program were seen as having a language deficiency. The bilingual program changed and was seen as serving the needs of students with a language deficiency. This motivated parents who spoke little or no English to enroll their children in the English-only classes instead of the bilingual education program. It seems that most parents considered the English-only instructional program the better option for ensuring academic success. However, teachers also report that limited English proficient (LEP) students who were enrolled in the English-only instructional track did not do as well on the assessment tests (e.g., TEAMS) as students who had gone through the bilingual program.

Elida Salinas points out that while the push for more English instruction came from teachers and administrators, there was also a push by community political groups that coincided with teacher sentiments. The political groups took form in the mid-1970s and continued until the 1979 elections. She states: "But after a while some people started, politics started to change and then we were having different political groups and those political groups would express dissatisfaction. Well, we don't like this, so they opposed the main group and that's how people started saying they don't want that much Spanish. Our children are supposed to be learning English." She adds that the state also passed new education policies that required school districts to teach essential elements and administer the TEAMS test: "I think it was the pressure from the state that really got the administrators to change . . . If you don't pass the TEAMS you don't graduate; you worry about that."

Linda Nieves recalls that a number of factors and forces impinged on teachers and students and thus influenced the structure and success of the program. Along with the internal factors discussed above, changes in the composition of the teaching staff contributed to the stability of the bilingual program:

> People would come and go and we'd have new faculty members . . . five of them would leave and we'd get five new ones, so I think all of that helped to say, hey, wait a minute the bilingual program isn't working. The kids need more English and then the parents started saying, my child is already in fifth grade and he can't read in English, and he can't read in Spanish. What's wrong? Some parents started saying well . . . my child can read in Spanish, but can he function when he goes to junior high school? Will he be able to function when he goes to junior high, high school and college?

Nora Matias, a third grade bilingual teacher before the program was restructured into a pre-K–first grade program, recalls parents expressing their concerns regarding the language of instruction: "The parents . . . were being very vocal. They wanted more English for their children. Some parents were . . . they would come to me and voice concerns saying one reason to send them to school was for them to speak English and Spanish." Matias adds that following the 1984–1985 program restructuring, school policy changed to the use of English in nonclassroom settings as well, such as the playground and cafeteria: "Little by little more concern is being vocalized and up to this point right now they encourage us as teachers, even as a whole staff, professional and everybody to speak informally to the kids. Not to punish them in some way if they do speak Spanish, but you know, encourage them to speak more English."

Rebecca Fernandez, a native of Cristal who received her university training in the field of bilingual education, was the first grade bilingual teacher at the time of my interview. She has taught in the bilingual program since the early 1980s when it was a maintenance program. She reflects on how the program has changed in the 1980s:

> It has changed since I've been teaching, you know, within the bilingual program. It has changed for the good. It wasn't very, like I said, too stable . . . there was criteria and everything, but, I guess, I wasn't very familiar with it and it was not very, I don't know what the word is that I'm trying to say. We didn't have, like, say now . . . where we have a, when the children have to meet these certain criteria to make the transition to English. We didn't have that before, we had the [Spanish language] readers, the children had to read and then. It was very, very, to be honest here, from the very beginning of the school year to the end of the school year the children were just in Spanish, they never made the transition. There was just Spanish throughout the whole year.

Fernandez adds that when the K-5 bilingual program was in operation students were expected to transition out of Spanish language instruction into English instruction by the end of third grade: "What I am saying is that when they got to third grade that's when they (other teachers) would start, well these children . . . they are very behind in their . . . reading, and of course, they went into the third grade class and they weren't going to get Spanish anymore."

The teachers cited above identify a number of factors and forces that precipitated the bilingual program reorganization. During the time that I conducted fieldwork in Crystal City (1988–1989), the teachers I interviewed generally agreed with the changes in the program and felt that the program was more efficient and served the needs of students. Very few teachers argued for maintenance bilingual/bicultural education. It was evident that the teachers embraced the transitional bilingual education ideology prevalent in the 1980s.

Many felt that the implementation of the transitional bilingual program was being administered more efficiently. Manriquez comments on this:

> I'm a firm believer in the program, in that theoretically speaking, I think it would be the best situation for the students . . . I would say that if bilingual education is to work, and to work you know as well as it should be intended to work, then I think that it needs to come down, first of all from the management or from the administrative point of the school. Everything has to be done to where that the teachers have access to better training methods, to methods of . . . to better periods of transition. This was one of the big questions I remember we had. When is a child going to meet a given criteria to reach a transition to go from a bilingual, a totally bilingual class to an English speaking class?

The emphasis on mastery and functioning in English is evident in most of the teacher narratives cited above. The discourse of cultural nationalism that was so prevalent during the *movimiento* was largely lacking when teachers talked about bilingual education. Most had adopted the ideology of transitional bilingual education and believed that acquiring English would facilitate entry into the mainstream society. Manriquez felt that the *movimiento* had been a struggle for greater integration and he believed that it was time for Cristal and Mexican Americans to go beyond an emphasis on cultural distinctiveness: "Let's get back into the mainstream, so that we can show everybody else we are just like other . . . just like every little town in the world or in the United States."

Conclusion

I argue that the school walkout served as a watershed moment for cultural production and the divergent formation of identities—some for, some against the new ideology of *Aztlán* and the proposed Chicano/Chicana educated person. The broader Chicano political movement *(el movimiento)*, which reached its height from the mid-1960s to the mid-1970s, provides the broader parameters for this analysis. Within this historical and cultural context, Chicano educators have played a prominent role in this development. The narrative excerpts that I have analyzed in this essay provide insight into the cultural, political, and social dynamics that have affected the lives and schooling experiences of teachers and students in this community. In this manner one can gain greater understanding of the relationship between Chicano cultural nationalism in relationship to the teaching ideology that took form in the 1970s at the school district level—the ideological framework guiding the cultural production of a Chicano/Chicana educated person.

I relied on interview data conducted among teachers in the school district in 1988–1989. My analysis focused on the relationship of *movimiento* ideology and the impact it had on teachers and their practice. I also looked at the relationship between the ideas and discourse of cultural nationalism, self-determination, and *Aztlán* in relationship to bilingual/bicultural education. My analysis shows that teachers' perspective of the school districts' teaching ideology that came in with the RUP in the 1970s changed during the 1980s due to numerous forces both within and outside the community. In pursuing this line of analysis, I show that schools are heterogeneous sites and the target of a variety of efforts to construct knowledge and identities. As a result, Chicano educators have had access to a variety of "voices" and practices, which has influenced their perspective on rejecting the "visionary" Chicano teaching ideology (in the form of maintenance bilingual/bicultural education); in turn, they adopted a transitional bilingual education program model that is more acceptable to the dominant socioideological formation of the nation-state.

Notes

1. Instead of following anthropological convention of using a pseudonym for the actual name of the community in order to maintain confidentiality, I decided to use the actual name, Crystal City. To ensure the confidentiality of my informants, I use pseudonyms for the actual people I interviewed. With respect to the use of ethnic labels, I use the terms Chicano, Mexicano, Mexican American, and Anglo-American. "Chicano" is a self-reference term used by ethnically and politically conscious Mexican Americans instead of terms such as Spanish American, Latin, Spanish surnamed, Hispanic, which have been used by the dominant society/culture to refer to members of this ethnic group. I use this term interchangeably with "Mexican American." "Mexicano" is the preferred self-identity term used by many Mexican Americans in South Texas, especially members of the older generation. In this chapter "Mexicano" is used interchangeably with Chicano and Mexican American, especially when emphasis is placed on the historical and cultural links of ethnicity. "Anglo-American" refers to members of the white mainstream population.

2. An earlier petition with seven demands, among them a call for establishing bilingual/bicultural education and signed by 350 students, was presented to the superintendent at the end of April 1969. The demand over equal representation of Anglo and Chicana cheerleaders had been met by the superintendent, who promised to institute a quota system of three Anglo and three Chicanas. The other demands, however, were stalled with a promise of being taken into consideration (Shockley 1974; see also *Zavala County Sentinel,* May 1, 1969).

3. For a discussion on the rise and fall of the Raza Unida Party, see García 1989 and Navarro 1998.

4. Crystal City became a major icon for the Chicano movement because it was one of the first communities where Chicanos took control of the governing institutions from the Anglo-American minority. Shockley (1974) covers changes in ethnic relations in the community since 1963, when a slate of five Mexicanos, referred to as Los Cinco, won the city council elections, defeating the Anglo administration. In 1965, the Anglo minority formed a coalition with more acculturated Mexican Americans to regain political power. In the city and school district elections of 1970, Mexicanos regained political control under the leadership of native son José Angel Gutiérrez and the RUP. Consequently, Crystal City came to represent the epitome of self-determination, and numerous Chicanos, engaged in political mobilization and education, looked at the success of this community as a model to emulate.

5. Within the Mexicano Spanish-speaking community Crystal City is often referred to as Cristal, a usage that I sometimes follow.

7. For a full discussion of the content and outcome of the twenty-two recommendations, see A. L. Trujillo, *Chicano Empowerment and Bilingual Education* (New York: Garland, 1998).

8. TEAMS was an integral part of HB 72, which was passed in 1984 by the Texas legislature. TEAMS was required in all Texas school districts and mandated that students be tested at the end of the first, third, fifth, seventh, ninth, and eleventh grades. The results of the tests were used to determine the percentage of students scoring at, above, and below grade level.

References

Barker, Chris, and Galasinski, Daruysz. 2001. *Cultural Studies and Discourse Analysis: A Dialogue on Language and Identity.* Thousand Oaks, CA: Sage.

Barth, F. 1969. *Ethnic Groups and Boundaries.* London: Allen & Unwin.

Bauman, Richard. 1977. *Verbal Art as Performance.* Prospect Heights, IL: Waveland.

Bogdan, Robert C., and Sari Knopp Biklen. 1982. *Qualitative Research for Education: An Introduction to Theory and Method.* Boston: Allyn & Bacon.

Brooker, P. 1999. *A Concise Glossary of Cultural Theory.* London: Arnold.

Camejo, Antonio, ed. 1971. *Documents of the Chicano Struggle.* New York: Pathfinder.

El Plan de Aztlán. 1971. http://latino.sscnet.ucla.edu/research/docs/struggle/aztlan.htm (retrieved February 17, 2003).

Emerson, R. M., R. I. Fretz, and L. L. Shaw. 1996. *Writing Ethnographic Notes.* Chicago: University of Chicago Press.

Erickson, Frederick. 1986. "Qualitative Methods in Research on Teaching." In *Handbook of Research on Teaching,* 3rd ed., ed. M. Whitrock, 119–61. New York: Macmillan.

Fairclough, N. 1995. *Critical Discourse Analysis: The Critical Study of Language.* London: Longman.

Foley, Douglas E. 1990. *Learning Capitalist Culture: Deep in the Heart of Tejas.* Philadelphia: University of Philadelphia Press.

Garcia, Ignacio. 1989. *United We Win: The Rise and Fall of La Raza Unida Party.* Tuscon: University of Arizona Press.

Gutiérrez, José Angel. 1998. *The Making of a Chicano Militant: Lessons from Cristal.* Madison: University of Wisconsin Press.

———. 1976. "Toward a Theory of Community Organization in a Mexican American Community in South Texas." Ph.D. diss., University of Texas.

Hall, Stuart. 1996. "New Ethnicities." In *Stuart Hall: Critical Dialogues in Cultural Studies,* ed. David Morley and D-K Chen, 441–49. London: Routledge.

Hardgrave, Robert L., and Santiago Hinojosa. 1975. *The Politics of Bilingual Education: A Study of Four Southwest Texas Communities.* Manchaca, TX: Sterling Swift.

Langenegger, Joy Ann. 1993. "The School as a Practical Tool: A Case Study of Crystal City, Texas." Master's thesis, Baylor University.

Levinson, Bradley A., and Dorothy C. Holland. 1996. "The Cultural Production of the Educated Person: An Introduction." In *The Cultural Production of the Educated Person: Critical Ethnographies of Schooling and Local Practice,* ed. B. A. Levinson, D. E. Foley, and D. C. Holland, 1–54. New York: State University of New York Press.

Melville, Margarita. 1983. "Ethnicity: An analysis of its dynamism and variability focusing on the Mexican/Anglo/Mexican American interface." *American Ethnologist* 10, no. 2: 272–89.

Navarro, Armando. 1998. *The Cristal Experiment: A Chicano Struggle for Community Control.* Madison: University of Wisconsin Press.

———. 1995. *Mexican American Youth Organization: Avant-Garde of the Chicano Movement in Texas.* Austin, TX: University of Texas Press.

Ogbu, John. 1981. "School Ethnography: A Multilevel Approach." *Anthropology and Education Quarterly* 12, no. 1: 3–29.

Padilla, Ray. 1984. "Federal Policy Shifts and the Implementation of Bilingual Education Programs." In *The Chicano Struggle: Analyses of Past and Present Efforts,* ed. R. T. Córdova and J. R. García, 90–110. Binghamton, NY: Bilingual Press/Editorial Bilingüe.

Post, Donald Eugene. 1975. "Ethnic Competition for Control of Schools in Two South Texas Towns." Ph.D. diss., University of Texas.

Reskin, Henry S., and Roger Williams. 1974. *The Schools of Cristal: An Experiment in Change.* Stanford, CA: Stanford Center for Research and Development in Teaching, Stanford University. Film.

Rosaldo, R. 1993. *Culture and Truth: The Remaking of Social Analysis.* Boston: Beacon.

Shockley, John Staples. 1974. *Chicano Revolt in a Texas Town.* Notre Dame, IN: University of Notre Dame Press.

Smith, Walter Elwood, Jr. 1978. "Mexican Resistance to Schooled Ethnicity: Ethnic Student Power in South Texas, 1930–1970." Ph.D. diss., University of Texas.

Smith, Walter Elwood, Jr., and Douglas E. Foley. 1978. "Mexican Resistance to Schooling in a South Texas Colony." *Education and Urban Society* 10, no. 2: 145–76.

———. 1975. *The Transition of Multiethnic Schooling in Model Town, Texas: 1930–1969.* Final Report NIE Project no. R020825 and no. 3-4003. Washington, DC: U.S. Department of Health, Education and Welfare, Office of Education.

Trujillo, Armando L. 1998. *Chicano Empowerment and Bilingual Education: Movimiento Politics in Crystal City, Texas.* New York: Garland.

Williams, Raymond. 1973. "Base and Superstructure in Marxist Cultural Theory." *New Left Review* 82: 3–16.

PART III

CHICANA AND MEXICANA MOTHERS' INVOLVEMENT WITH CHILDREN, FAMILY, AND POLITICS

5

Exploring Parental Involvement among Mexican American and Latina Mothers

Robert P. Moreno

QUALITY EDUCATION AND CHILDREN'S ACADEMIC SUCCESS have been long-standing national concerns. This is particularly the case for Mexican Americans and other Latinos whose educational achievement lags behind the rest of the nation. For example, according to recent figures the dropout rate for Latinos (28.6 percent) is considerably higher than for black or white non-Latinos (12.6 percent and 7.3 percent respectively) (Rumberger and Rodríguez 2002). One response to this educational crisis has been a call for increased parental involvement. In general, educational researchers have argued that parental involvement can serve as a major tool to curtail school failure and promote academic success (Coleman 1987; Epstein 1990; Oakes and Lipton 1990; Hoover-Dempsey et al. 1987). Unfortunately, few of the studies that have focused on the prevalence and efficacy of parent involvement have included Mexican Americans and other Latino subgroups.

More recently, however, qualitative researchers have taken a more in-depth look at parental involvement and how it pertains to Mexican American and other Latino families. These researchers have suggested that our traditional understandings of parental involvement may be less appropriate for Latinos due to the unique characteristics of the population. For example, Mexican Americans and other Latinos struggle with language barriers, limited family resources, differing cultural values, and family interaction patterns as compared to their mainstream counterparts (Delgado-Gaitan 1990; Gándara 1995; López, Scribner, and Mahitivanichcha 2001; Moreno 1997, 2002; Valdés 1996). This research has pointed the way to identifying the unique factors that may affect the capacity of Mexican American and other Latino families to participate in their children's education.

Drawing from previous research, the objective of this chapter is twofold: (1) to investigate the factors that predict parental involvement among Latina mothers and (2) to explore the impact of the involvement on their children's educational outcomes.

Overview of Parental Involvement

The general literature on parental involvement suggests there are a number of variables that may influence parents' desire or ability to participate in their children's schooling. To better understand these multiple influences, I have taken an ecological perspective to organizing the literature (Bronfenbrenner 1986). I have classified the research findings into three general categories: personal/psychological, contextual, and sociodemographic.

Personal and psychological variables are personal beliefs or characteristics that parents may possess that can influence his or her behavior, and thereby impact their child's development. For example, research has shown that parents with high expectations for their children's educational attainment are more likely to involve themselves in their schooling (Henderson 1981; Hess and Holloway 1984; Soto 1988). Similarly, parents who perceive themselves as competent regarding school matters tend to become more involved in their children's education as compared to their less competent counterparts (Hess 1969; Schaefer and Edgerton 1985; Swick 1987, 1988). However, the relationship between parental efficacy and parent involvement has not been widely studied among Mexican Americans and other Latinos. This is problematic because of the relatively low level of educational attainment among Latinos and the positive association between parental efficacy and parental schooling attainment (Swick 1988). In addition, Latino parents' level of acculturation may influence their level of familiarity with their children's schools and their roles as parents within these schools (Delgado-Gaitan 1990; Stevenson et al. 1990). Latino parents' lack of familiarity with the U.S. educational system may also influence their efficacy beliefs regarding involvement in their children's schooling.

Parents' knowledge about school activities, procedures, and policies are also an important factor. Simply put, parents who are more knowledgeable about school activities are more likely to be involved in these types of activities (Delgado-Gaitan 1990; Klimes-Dougan et al. 1992). However, the link between parents' knowledge and involvement can be more complicated for Latino parents who are limited in their ability to speak English and where schools personnel are limited in their ability to speak Spanish. In this case, a "knowledge gap" may be created as a result of a "language gap" between Latino parents and their children's schools (Moreno and Lopez 1999).

Finally, the way in which parents understand their responsibilities with respect to their child's education is crucial to their involvement. For example, parents may have high educational expectations for their children, but they are less likely to involve themselves in their children's schooling if they do not believe that it is their responsibility to do so. In general, parents who believe that they should be involved in their children's education are more likely to report being involved in their children's education than parents who do not accept this role definition (Meighan 1989; Schaefer and Edgerton 1985; Sigel 1985).

The second group of research findings falls into the contextual category. These findings are based on the perspective that "the way one perceives his surroundings or environment influences the way one will behave in that environment" (Insel and Moos 1974, 179). For example, parents' level of involvement may be facilitated or inhibited by the nature and number of barriers their context affords. These contextual barriers may be of a practical nature (e.g., conflicting work schedules of parents and teachers, childcare transportation, etc.) or an institutional nature (e.g., lack of provision of bilingual staff, inadequate training of teachers, inadequate resources to support parent involvement) (Adelman 1991). In addition, educational researchers argue that schools create and maintain particular "climates" which can influence parents' involvement in their children's school (Haynes, Comer, and Hamilton-Lee 1989). This is also the case for the families themselves. Familial and other social support systems enable parents to involve themselves in their children's schooling (Clark 1983; Epstein 1990). However, the influence of social support and parent involvement has not been well studied among Latinos. This gap is important because there is a positive relationship between levels of social support, socioeconomic, and acculturation level. For example, Mexican Americans with higher acculturation and educational levels report larger social support networks and more frequent contact with their network members than Mexican Americans with lower levels of acculturation and education (Griffith and Villavicencio 1985).

In addition to the more malleable personal and contextual factors, sociodemographic factors have been shown to be important in understanding parents' level of participation in their children's education. For example, several researchers have suggested that ethnicity and/or race is an important indicator of parents' level of involvement. Lynch and Stein (1987) found that Latino parents reported significantly lower levels of involvement in their children's educational planning decisions when compared to their African American and non-Hispanic white counterparts. Similarly, Stevenson, Chen, and Uttal (1990) found that—despite having very positive attitudes toward their children's schooling—Latino mothers reported being less involved in their children's schooling than African American and non-Hispanic white parents. Similarly, research has consistently found that parents from middle- and high-socioeconomic backgrounds are more likely to participate in their children's education than parents from low socioeconomic backgrounds (Epstein 1990; Hoover-Dempsey et al. 1987; Lareau 1987, 1989; Stevenson, Chen, and Uttal 1990). Moreover, maternal education has been shown to be a particularly important variable for understanding teaching interactions in the home among Mexican Americans (Laosa 1982; Moreno 1997). Laosa (1982) argues persuasively that maternal education is often a better indicator of education-related activities than broader measures like socioeconomic status.

Finally, a sociodemographic variable that is often ignored is acculturation. Although it is of minimal importance for the vast majority of whites, it is crucial for understanding Mexican Americans and other Latinos. While the specific nature of the acculturation process is hotly debated, psychologists understand the process as a change that occurs when individuals are exposed to a new culture and cultural learning and behavioral adaptation takes place (Marín and Marín 1991). Acculturation involves changes in cognition, language, and interpersonal interactions, and has been shown to be a key construct for understanding Latinos across a number of psychological, social, economic, and political contexts (Rueschenberg and Buriel 1989; Marín and Marín 1991). The single most robust index of acculturation is language use and preference. In the case of Mexican Americans and other Latinos in the United States, the degree to which one prefers and uses Spanish or English correlates highly with the degree to which one embraces the values and behaviors of the U.S. mainstream.

Although the research on parental involvement is extensive, much of it is incomplete with respect to Mexican Americans and other Latinos. Building on the current body of research, the objective of this chapter is to investigate the personal/psychological, contextual, and sociodemographic factors that predict parental involvement among Latina mothers and to explore the impact of their involvement on their children's educational outcomes.

The Study

The participants consisted of 158 mothers who were the primary care providers of their first grade children. The mothers were recruited from elementary schools in the Los Angeles area. The mothers varied by socioeconomic backgrounds and ethnicity (see tables 5.1 and 5.2). The mothers were interviewed in their preferred language (English or Spanish) by trained bilingual interviewers. The interview consisted of an eighty-item questionnaire that required thirty to forty-five minutes to complete. Drawing on previous research, the interview comprised five general areas: (1) sociodemographic, (2) personal/psychological, (3) contextual, (4) mothers' level of involvement in their children's schooling, and (5) social desirability.[1]

Sociodemographic

To obtain the relevant background information, all participants were asked to provide information on their age, marital status, number of children and adults in the home, the educational and occupational level of the respondent and her spouse/partner, length of residence in the United States, and their acculturation status.

Personal/Psychological

To assess the mothers' attitudes and perceptions toward involvement in their children's schooling, each participant was questioned regarding four specific areas. The first of these was *role definition* (Schaefer and Edgerton 1985). Mothers were queried regarding their attitudes toward their role in their children's educational development (i.e., "What I teach my child at home is very important to her/his school success."). In addition, the participants were asked about their *perceived efficacy* (Johnston and Mash 1989); that is, mothers were questioned about their expectations for successfully coping with parenting situations (i.e., "Helping my child with homework is easy for me."). Another important area included *school knowledge*. School knowledge consisted of a series of questions asking parents about their knowledge regarding the presence of common school-related activities (i.e., "Do you usually hear about different programs that the school offers to parents; . . . know about the school advisory

TABLE 5.1
Demographic Characteristics of Latina Mothers

	Mean	Standard Deviation
Mother's age	32.8	6.2
Number of children	3.0	1.3
Mother's years in school	9.5	2.7
Adults living in the home	2.4	1.2
Years in the United States	20.6	7.18

N = 158

council?"). Finally, mothers were asked about their *educational expectations* for their child ("How will your child do in school next year? Or "How much schooling do you expect your child to receive?") (Seginer 1983).

Contextual Factors

In addition to the personal/psychological area, information was gathered regarding the mothers' perception of contextual factors relevant to parent involvement. These included school climate, social support, and barriers.

School climate consisted of a measure of the parents' perceptions of the school environment (i.e., "I think people in this school care about me as a person.").

Social support assessed the perceptions of assistance parents received from family members and friends regarding school involvement. Mothers were asked to identify the number of individuals who provide assistance (i.e., family members and friends). Of those who were indicated to provide assistance, mothers were asked to indicate the frequency of the help (Griffith and Villavicencio 1985).

Finally, mothers were queried about any perceived barriers to parental involvement. In doing so, mothers were first asked whether they experienced difficulty being involved in their children's education. If a mother answered yes, then the interviewer read a list of nine common problems (e.g., work schedule, difficulty in arranging child care, don't feel safe in the school/neighborhood). The mother was then asked to indicate which problems she encountered that made it difficult for her to be involved.

Mothers' Level of Involvement

A two-step process was used to assess the mothers' level of involvement. First, mothers were asked if they participated in the various involvement activities (e.g., "Do you call or stop to speak with your child's teacher without an appointment?" "Do you attend school PTA or school advisory meetings?"). The measure included two activities from five types of parent involvement (see Epstein 1990). If the mothers' response was yes to any activity, they were then asked how often. This procedure yielded two involvement scores, quantity and frequency. The *quantity* of involvement measured the types of activities in which the mothers participated (i.e., basic obligation, communication, involvement at school, learning at home, and school governance). The *frequency* of involvement measured how often they engaged in each type of activity.

Children's School Outcomes

In addition to the mothers' responses to the structured interview, these data were gathered on the children's school performance in four areas: academic grades, behavior grades, total number of school absences, and total number of school tardies. These data were collected from the students' permanent records.

Social Desirability

Finally, in an effort to measure the extent to which the respondents answered in a socially desirable manner, a short version of the Marlowe-Crowne Social Desirability Scale was used (Reynolds 1982).

Results

The first part of the analysis assessed the extent of the mothers' involvement. As table 5.3 indicates, the mothers reported involvement at all levels. Virtually all the mothers reported some participation with respect to "basic obligations" (99.3 percent), communication between home and school (94.1 percent), and learning activities at home (99.4 percent). However, a majority of the mothers reported (57.5 percent) no involvement at the school site, and just over half (55.9 percent) reported that they engaged in some type of "governance" activity. The mean quantity of involvement was 6.1 (standard deviation = 1.68). Similarly, the mothers' frequency of involvement ranged from a mean of 3.85 for "basic obligations" to a mean of 2.50 for "governance." The mean frequency of involvement was 3.13 (standard deviation = .90).

Predicting Parental Involvement

The second part of the analysis assessed which variables predicted the nature and frequency of parental involvement. Two stepwise multiple

TABLE 5.2
Latina Mothers' Ethnicity

Mexican American	78%
Central American	15%
South American	1%
Other	6%

TABLE 5.3
Mothers' Involvement by Type (%) and
Frequency (Mean and Standard Deviation)

	Some Participation	Frequency
Basic Obligation	99.3	3.85 (.45)
Communication	94.1	3.14 (.85)
Involvement at School	42.5	2.74 (.85)
Learning at Home	99.4	3.57 (.83)
School Governance	55.9	2.50 (.73)

regression analyses were conducted. In each analysis, the "social desirability" measure was forced into equation to control for response bias. Tables 5.4 and 5.5 show the results of the analysis. Of the eleven variables entered in the model (i.e., acculturation, socioeconomic status, family composition, school-related knowledge, perceived efficacy, role definition, educational expectations, spousal support, barriers to involvement, school climate, and family cohesion), only three accounted for a significant portion of the variance (27 percent) with respect to quantity of involvement. These included spouse support (14 percent), knowledge of school activities (11 percent), and SES (2 percent). Thus mothers who reported that they were more knowledgeable regarding school activities, who had spouses who were supportive, and had a higher SES were more likely to participate in a larger variety of parental involvement activities. Similarly, only four variables accounted for a significant portion of the variance (25 percent) with respect to frequency of involvement. As table 5.5 shows, mothers who reported that they experienced fewer barriers, had spouses who were supportive, viewed themselves as important to their child's education, and were knowledgeable about school activities were more likely to participate more frequently in parental involvement activities.

Predicting Children's School Outcomes

The third part of the analyses addressed the influence of parental involvement on children's school outcomes. The analyses were conducted in several steps.

TABLE 5.4
Summary of Stepwise Multiple Regression Analyses Predicting
Latina Mothers' Quantity of Parental Involvement

Step	Variable Entered	Partial R^2	Model R^2	F	p
0	Social desirability	.00	.00	.54	.46
1	Spousal support	.13	.14	23.32	.00
2	School knowledge	.11	.24	21.58	.00
3	Socioeconomic status	.02	.27	4.35	.04
4	Educational expectations	.01	.28	2.79	.09

TABLE 5.5
Summary of Stepwise Multiple Regression Analyses Predicting
Latina Mothers' Frequency of Parental Involvement

Step	Variable Entered	Partial R²	Model R²	F	P
0	Social desirability	.00	.00	.07	.79
1	Barriers	.14	.14	24.99	.00
2	Spousal support	.05	.19	8.65	.00
3	Role definition	.04	.22	6.76	.01
4	School knowledge	.03	.25	5.02	.02
5	Perceived efficacy	.02	.26	3.22	.07

First, due to the limited availability of children's outcome data, the sample size decreased from 158 to 109. To reduce the number of predictor variables for multiple regression analyses, zero-order correlations were computed among the thirteen possible predictor variables and the four children's school outcome variables. Predictor variables that did not correlate significantly with any of the four children's outcome variables were excluded from further analyses (see table 5.6).

Next, a series of four stepwise multiple regression analyses were conducted to determine the overall contributions of the remaining independent variables on each of the children's school outcome variables. Again, in each analysis "social desirability" was "forced" into equation to control for response bias.

As seen in table 5.7, of the eight variables included in the model (i.e., acculturation, family composition, school-related knowledge, educational

TABLE 5.6
Zero-Order Correlations between the Independent Variables
and Children's School Outcomes

	Academic Grades	Behavior Grades	School Absences	School Tardies
Acculturation	.21*	.16	.34***	.23**
Family composition	−.10	.01	−.30***	−.20*
School knowledge	.10	.06	.20*	.22**
Schooling expectation	−.01	−.05	−.09	−.21*
Spousal support	.08	.03	−.24**	−.10
Barriers	.02	.01	−.20*	.01
School climate	.06	−.05	.19*	.03
Quantity of involvement	.02	.07	−.22**	−.02
SES	.09	.15	−.03	.13
Perceived efficacy	.02	.12	.13	−.07
Role definition	.07	.00	.12	.09
Family cohesion	−.01	.10	.03	.08
Frequency of involvement	−.05	.06	−.04	.02

*p < .05 **p < .01 ***p < .001

TABLE 5.7
Stepwise Multiple Regression Analyses
Predicting Children's Academic Grades

Step	Variable Entered	Partial R^2	Model R^2	F	P
0	Social desirability	.00	.00	.01	.92
1	Acculturation	.06	.06	6.54	.01

expectations, spousal support, barriers, school climate, quantity of involvement), only the mothers' level of acculturation accounted for a significant portion of the variance when predicting children's academic grades. Mothers who were more acculturated had children with higher grades. No significant model was found for children's behavioral grades (see table 5.8).

As for nonacademic outcomes, the analysis shows that mothers' acculturation and level of spousal support were significant predictors of their children's school absences (see table 5.9). Mothers who were more acculturated and had a supportive spouse had children with fewer absences. Similarly, mothers who were more acculturated had children with fewer tardies (see table 5.10).

Discussion

The results of the study indicate several important findings. First, our analysis shows that the mothers' level of involvement in their children's schooling ranged widely, depending on the nature of the involvement. Mexican American and other Latina mothers, were highly engaged in home-based activities (i.e., "basic obligations," "communication," "learning at home"). However, their participation in school site activities (i.e., involvement at school, school governance) was lower. These results are consistent with the previous research that also found that Latinos tend to be less engaged in involvement activities at the school (Bermudez and

TABLE 5.8
Stepwise Multiple Regression Analyses
Predicting Children's Behavior Grades

Step	Variable Entered	Partial R^2	Model R^2	F	P
0	Social desirability	.00	.00	.25	.61
1	Acculturation	.02	.02	2.40	.12

TABLE 5.9
Stepwise Regression Analyses Predicting Children's School Absences

Step	Variable Entered	Partial R^2	Model R^2	F	P
0	Social desirability	.01	.01	1.37	.24
1	Acculturation	.11	.12	12.82	.00
2	Spousal support	.05	.17	6.60	.01
3	School climate	.02	.19	2.74	.10

Padron 1988; Chavkin and Williams 1989; Delgado-Gaitan 1990, 1991; Epstein 1990; Klimes-Dougan et al. 1992; Goldenberg 1987). These findings stress that when educators evaluate the level of parent involvement among Latinos, it is important to differentiate among the various types of parental involvement. This is particularly important given that Latinos are involved in activities that are least visible to teachers and school administrators. For example, a teacher is more likely to notice the absent mother at the parent-teacher conference and miss the emphasis she places on schooling at home. This, in turn, can lead school officials to draw inaccurate views of Latino parents such as "they don't care about their children's education."

Turning our attention to the factors that predict parental involvement, the picture becomes more complex. First, our findings show that combinations of factors are associated with Latina mothers' involvement in their children's schooling. Mothers who had greater spousal support, more school-related knowledge, and higher socioeconomic status participated in a wider array of parental involvement activities. A similar pattern was found for frequency of involvement. Once again the presence of spousal support and knowledge about school activities were important. However, the presence of barriers such as a difficult work schedule, limited child care, and so on, and the mothers' role definitions were also important predictors. Thus mothers with more supportive environments (spousal support and fewer barriers) and personal resources (school-oriented role and knowledge) participated in parental involvement activities more frequently. Interestingly, mothers'

TABLE 5.10
Stepwise Regression Analyses Predicting Children's School Tardiness

Step	Variable Entered	Partial R^2	Model R^2	F	P
0	Social desirability	.01	.01	1.40	.24
1	Acculturation	.05	.06	5.12	.02
2	Spousal knowledge	.02	.08	2.62	.10

socioeconomic status was not a contributing factor with respect to the frequency of involvement.

When we examine the predictors of Latino parental involvement, the findings support an ecological perspective (Bronfenbrenner 1986). Personal, contextual, and sociodemographic factors all play a role in understanding Latina involvement. At the personal level, more involved Latina mothers have important interpersonal tools; they tend to view themselves as important to their children's education and are more knowledgeable about school activities. More involved Latina mothers also reside in a more facilitating context at the immediate family level, as well as the broader school and community level. Involved mothers have more supportive spouses and face fewer barriers (i.e., transportation, child care, etc.). At the sociodemographic level, mothers who have higher socioeconomic status are also more likely to be involved in a wider array of involvement activities.

Contextual and personal factors appear to be more critical in indicating the extent and frequency in which Latina mothers are involved. Our analysis shows that low socioeconomic status is not an overwhelming constraint to Latina involvement. By including both the mothers' socioeconomic status and contextual barriers in our analysis, we gained a clearer picture of what is going on. The data suggest that although both are important, barriers such as a difficult work schedule and/or a lack of child care are more likely to impede involvement than limited resources that result from less education and income. Put another way, regardless of socioeconomic status, Latina mothers tend to maintain their involvement in their children's schooling. This is not to say that Latino families with limited resources do not experience more difficulty in maintaining their involvement level, but rather, regardless of the difficulty, they maintain their involvement. This is important to note because it attests to the importance that limited resource Latino families place on involvement activities.

These findings echo those of previous researchers who argue that low levels of involvement among Latino parents may be due to several factors: poor communication between the family and the school, lack of familiarity with their role vis-à-vis their children's education, and personal and institutional barriers (Adelman 1991; Bermudez and Padron 1988; Delgado-Gaitan 1990; Goldenberg 1987; Klimes-Dougan et al. 1992; Nieto 1985). Moreover, the data suggest that when parent involvement is low, it is the school-based activities that tend to suffer. Home-based involvement tends to stay constant.

When we address the question, What is the relationship between parental involvement and children's school outcomes? the results are surprising. In contrast to prior studies, we found limited support for a positive relationship between Latina involvement and their children's school outcomes. Interestingly, our analysis did not show that mothers who engaged in more parental involvement activities had children who performed better academically or were better behaved. Although we found some evidence that mothers who engaged in more parental involvement had children with fewer absences, this did not hold up in the subsequent analyses. Rather, it was the mothers' acculturation level that was the most consistent indicator of children's school performance (academic and behavioral grades, and attendance).

The reason for this is not clear. One explanation lies in the acculturation measure used. The scale indexes an individual's acculturation by way of language preference and use (i.e., "In general, what language do you speak?"). Although the measure is administered to the mother, we believe it also indexes the English language use and proficiency of the child. If we are correct, then the data suggest that children who are less acculturated (are less proficient in English) do worse in school, compared to their more acculturated counterparts, regardless of their mothers' level of parental involvement. Thus parental involvement may have a limited impact on the children's educational achievement for limited English proficiency families—at least in the short term. At this early stage in children's educational career (i.e., first grade), their English language proficiency is more likely to impact their grade than the mothers' level of parental involvement activity.

This is not to say that parental involvement for Mexican Americans and other Latinos is void of value. It may be that over the course of a child's educational career a continuous pattern of parent involvement may facilitate positive school outcomes. However, the development and maintenance of Latino parent involvement requires a comprehensive effort on the part of both the schools and parents. Schools and parents must communicate with each other to establish supportive familial and educational environments by discussing and negotiating their respective roles in the educational process of their children and by removing the barriers (i.e., transportation, child care, etc.) that impede involvement. Moreover, schools must be careful to recognize both home-based and school-based involvement activities. Our findings caution us against a simplistic notion that parental involvement directly corresponds to children's immediate academic achievement. Rather, our understanding of parental involvement must include a more long-term approach to engaging families. In the short term, parental involvement may not compensate for more direct educational interventions such as bilingual education programs for limited English-speaking children and their families.

Note

I extend my thanks and gratitude to Jose A. Lopez, whose efforts made this chapter possible.

1. For a more detailed description of the variables, see Moreno and Lopez 1999.

References

Adelman, Howard. 1991. "Parents and Schools: An Intervention Perspective." Paper presented at the American Psychological Association, San Francisco, August 16–22.

Bandura, Albert. 1977. "Self-Efficacy: Toward a Unifying Theory of Behavioral Change." *Psychological Review* 84, no. 2: 191–215.

Bermudez, Andrea B., and Yolanda N. Padron. 1988. "University–School Collaboration That Increases Minority Parent Involvement." *Educational Horizons* 66, no. 2: 83–86.

Bronfenbrenner, Urie. 1979. *The Ecology of Human Development.* Cambridge: Harvard University Press.

———. 1986. "Ecology of the Family as a Context for Human Development: Research Perspectives." *Developmental Psychology* 22, no. 6: 723–42.

Chapa, Jorge, and Richard R. Valencia. 1993. "Latino Population Growth, Demographic Characteristics, and Educational Stagnation: An Examination of Recent Trends." *Hispanic Journal of Behavioral Sciences* 15, no. 2: 165–87.

Chavkin, Nancy F., and David L. Williams. 1989. "Low-Income Parents' Attitudes toward Parent Involvement in Education." *Journal of Sociology & Social Welfare* 16, no. 3: 17–28.

Clark, Reginald. 1983. *Family Life and School Achievement: Why Poor Black Children Succeed or Fail.* Chicago: University of Chicago Press.

Coleman, James S. 1987. "Families and Schools." *Educational Researcher* 16, no. 6: 32–38.

Delgado-Gaitan, Concha. 1990. *Literacy for Empowerment: The Role of Parents in Children's Education.* New York: Falmer.

———. 1991. "Involving Parents in the Schools: A Process of Empowerment." *American Journal of Education* 100, no. 1: 20–46.

Epstein, Joyce L. 1990. "School and Family Connections: Theory, Research, and Implications for Integrating Sociologies of Education and Family." *Marriage and Family Review* 15, no. 1–2: 99–126.

Gándara, Patricia C. 1995. *Over the Ivy Walls: The Educational Mobility of Low-Income Chicanos.* Albany: State University of New York Press.

Goldenberg, Claude N. 1987. "Low-Income Hispanic Parents' Contributions to their First-Grade Children's Word-Recognition Skills." *Anthropology & Education Quarterly* 18, no. 3: 149–79.

Griffith, James, and Sandra Villavicencio. 1985. "Relationships among Acculturation, Sociodemographic Characteristics, and Social Supports in Mexican American Adults." *Hispanic Journal of Behavioral Sciences* 7, no. 1: 75–92.

Haynes, Norris M., James P. Comer, and Muriel Hamilton-Lee. 1989. "School Climate Enhancement through Parent Involvement." *Journal of School Psychology* 27, no. 1: 87–90.

Henderson, Ronald W. 1981. "Home Environment and Intellectual Performance." In *Parent–Child Interaction: Theory, Research, and Prospects*, ed. Ronald W. Henderson. New York: Academic Press.

Hess, Robert. 1969. "Parental Behavior and Children's School Achievement: Implications for Head Start." In *Critical Issues in Research Related to Disadvantaged Children*, ed. E. Grotberg, 1–76. Princeton, NJ: Educational Testing Services.

Hess, Robert, and Susan D. Holloway. 1984. "Family and School as Educational Institutions." In *Review of Child Development Research*. Vol. 7. *The Family*, ed. R. D. Parke, 179–222. Chicago: University of Chicago Press.

Hoover-Dempsey, Kathleen V., Otto C. Bassler, and Jane S. Brissie. 1987. "Parent Involvement: Contributions of Teacher Efficacy, School Socioeconomic Status, and other School Characteristics." *American Educational Research Journal* 24, no. 3: 417–35.

Insel, Paul M., and Rudolph H. Moos. 1974. "Psychological Environments: Expanding the Scope of Human Ecology." *American Psychologist* 29, no. 3: 179–88.

Johnston, Charlotte, and Eric J. Mash. 1989. "A Measure of Parenting Satisfaction and Efficacy." *Journal of Clinical Child Psychology* 18, no. 2: 167–75.

Klimes-Dougan, Bonnie, Jose A. Lopez, Howard S. Adelman, and Patricia Nelson. 1992. "Two Studies of Low Income Parents' Involvement in Schooling." *Urban Review* 24, no. 3: 185–202.

Laosa, Luis M. 1982. "School, Occupation, Culture, and Family: The Impact of Parental Schooling on the Parent-Child Relationship." *Journal of Educational Psychology* 74, no. 6: 791–827.

Lareau, Annette. 1987. "Social Class Differences in Family-School Relationships: The Importance of Cultural Capital." *Sociology of Education* 60, no. 2: 73–85.

———. 1989. *Home Advantage: Social Class and Parental Intervention in Elementary Education*. London: Falmer.

López, Gerardo, R., Jay D. Scribner, and Kanya Mahitivanichcha. 2001. "Redefining Parental Involvement: Lessons from High-Performing Migrant-Impacted Schools." *American Educational Research Journal* 38, no. 2: 253–88.

Lynch, Eleanor W., and Robert C. Stein. 1987. "Parent Participation by Ethnicity: A Comparison of Hispanic, Black, and Anglo Families." *Exceptional Children* 54, no. 2: 105–11.

Marín, Gerardo, and Barbara VanOss Marín. 1991. *Research with Hispanic Populations*. Newbury Park, CA: Sage.

Meighan, Roland. 1989. "The Parents and the Schools: Alternative Role Definitions." *Educational Review* 41, no. 2: 105–12.

Moreno, Robert P. 1997. "Everyday Instruction: A Comparison of Mexican American and Anglo Mothers and Their Preschool Children." *Hispanic Journal of Behavioral Sciences* 19, no. 4: 527–39.

———. 2002. "Teaching the Alphabet: An Exploratory Look at Maternal Instruction in Mexican American Families." *Hispanic Journal of Behavioral Sciences* 24, no. 2: 191–205.

Moreno, Robert P., and Jose A. Lopez. 1999. "The Role of Acculturation and Maternal Education in Latina Mothers' Involvement in Their Children's Schooling." *School Community Journal* 9, no. 1: 83–101.

National Center for Education Statistics. 1990. *Elementary and Secondary Education.* Vol. 1. U.S. Department of Education Office of Educational Research and Improvement. Washington, DC: U.S. Government Printing Office.

National Commission on Excellence in Education. 1983. *A Nation at Risk: The Imperative for Educational Reform.* Washington, DC: U.S. Government Printing Office.

National Commission on Secondary Education for Hispanics. 1984. *Make Something Happen: Hispanics and Urban High School.* Washington, DC: Hispanic Policy Development Project.

Nieto, Sonia. 1985. "Who's Afraid of Bilingual Parents?" *Bilingual Review* 12, no. 3: 179–89.

Oakes, Jeannie, and Martin Lipton. 1990. *Making the Best of Schools: A Handbook for Parents, Teachers, and Policy Makers.* New Haven: Yale University Press.

Reynolds, William M. 1982. "Development of Reliable and Valid Short Forms of the Marlowe-Crowne Social Desirability Scale." *Journal of Clinical Psychology* 38, no. 1: 119–25.

Rueschenberg, Erich, and Raymond Buriel. 1989. "Mexican American Family Functioning and Acculturation: A Family Systems Perspective." *Hispanic Journal of Behavioral Sciences* 11, no. 3: 232–44.

Rumberger, Russell W., and Gloria M. Rodríguez. 2002. "Chicano Dropouts: An Update of Research and Policy Issues." In *Chicano School Failure and Success: Past, Present, and Future,* ed. Richard R. Valencia, 114–46. New York: Routledge Falmer.

Schaefer, E. S., and M. Edgerton. 1985. "Parent and Child Correlates of Parental Modernity." In *Parental Belief Systems: The Psychological Consequences for Children,* ed. Irving E. Sigel, 287–318. Hillsdale, NJ: Lawrence Erlbaum, 1985.

Seginer, Rachel. 1983. "Parents' Educational Expectations and Children's Academic Achievement: A Literature Review." *Merrill-Palmer Quarterly* 29, no. 1: 1–23.

Sigel, M. 1985. "A Study of Maternal Beliefs and Values within the Context of an Intervention Program." In *Parental Belief Systems: The Psychological Consequences for Children,* ed. Irving E. Sigel, 271–86. Hillsdale, NJ: Lawrence Erlbaum.

Soto, Lourdes D. 1988. "The Home Environment of Higher and Lower Achieving Puerto Rican Children." *Hispanic Journal of Behavioral Sciences* 10, no. 2: 161–67.

Stevenson, Harold W., Chuansheng Chen, and David H. Uttal. 1990. "Beliefs and Achievement: A Study of Black, White, and Hispanic Children." *Child Development* 61, no. 2: 508–23.

Swick, Kevin J. 1987. "Teacher Reports on Parental Efficacy/Involvement Relationships." *Journal of Instructional Psychology* 14: 125–32.

———. 1988. "Parental Efficacy and Involvement: Influences on Children." *Childhood Education* 65, no. 1: 37–42.

Valdés, Guadalupe. 1996. *Con Respeto: Bridging the Distances between Culturally Diverse Families and Schools.* New York: Teachers College Press.

6

Chicana Teen Mothers: Acculturation, Social Support, and Perceptions of Motherhood

Elsa O. Valdez

S INCE 1994, LATINA TEENS HAVE HAD THE HIGHEST TEEN BIRTHRATE AMONG the major racial/ethnic groups in the United States. For the year 2000, the birthrate for Latinas fifteen to nineteen years old was 94.4 per 1,000, nearly double the national rate of 48.7 per 1,000 (National Campaign to Prevent Teen Pregnancy 2001). If we examine teen birthrates among Latino subgroups, we find that fifteen- to nineteen-year-old Mexican Americans had the highest teen birthrate (101.5 per 1,000), followed by Latina teens of other/unknown origin (including Central and South American) with a birthrate of 81.3 per 1,000, followed closely by Puerto Rican teens with a birthrate of 79.7 per 1,000 (National Campaign to Prevent Teen Pregnancy 2001).

This chapter will examine the interrelationships between acculturation, generation in the United States, social support networks (instrumental and emotional support), adjustment and perceptions of motherhood, and self-esteem among Chicana teen mothers. In-depth interviews with thirty Chicana teen mothers provide us with an opportunity to learn more about a group that has historically been ignored in the social sciences and routinely depicted in the media as deviant or lacking morals. Three key questions guide this study: (1) What are Chicana adolescent mothers' perceptions of motherhood? (2) Is there a connection between social support networks and self-esteem? (3) How do acculturation and generation affect social support networks?

Purpose of Study

This study is important for two reasons. First, there have been major demographic changes over the past decade, which need to be monitored and examined by policy makers, social service providers, and research scientists. For example, the Mexican-origin population increased from 13.5 million in 1990 to 20.6 million in 2000 (Saenz, Morales, and Filoteo 2004). More than one-third of the nation's 35 million Latinos are under eighteen years of age, and Mexicans are the Latino subgroup with the youngest median age (Perez 2001, 12). As noted previously, the rates for Latina teen mothers tend to be very high. Thus it is imperative that we pay attention to the effects of changing demographics on the quality of life for Chicana/Latina adolescent mothers and their families. A second reason is that research focused on Latina adolescent mothers tends to be scant and is often pejorative. We know very little about the lives of these young women and their families. Consequently, social policy is often based on notions of cultural determinism, which implies that children of unwed mothers are destined to lifelong poverty and/or criminal activity. Most studies of communities focus on risk factors associated with demographic characteristics and physical environment, and pay less attention to the social processes that protect youth, such as informal social networks and protective cultural norms (Denner et al. 2001).

Theoretical Framework

Among the various perspectives of adolescent motherhood, the culture of poverty view tends to be the most pejorative and politically powerful model. In the culture of poverty rendition, the institution of single-mother families reproduces attitudes, behaviors, and values permitting teenage sexual promiscuity and reliance on welfare (Kaplan 1997). This one-dimensional framework tends to focus on supposed "cultural specific" characteristics without examining the effects of race, class, and gender. A second framework is the alternative life course or cultural strategies model (Franklin 1992; Hamberg and Dickson 1992; Staples 1985; Stack 1974; Ladner 1972). According to this view, early parenthood is an adaptive response to harsh living conditions such as poverty, low levels of education, and high rates of unemployment. Given their marginal position, young, poor, urban women, such as African Americans and Latinas, choose to become single mothers because they have limited life course options. While this view explains how various structural factors (e.g., race and class) push young minority women into early parenthood, as well as subsequent strategies that adolescent mothers utilize to cope with being a teen parent, this model fails to acknowledge the effects of gender. For example, females are socialized to idealize certain roles, such as being a nurturing mother. The internalization of ideal female virtues happens early in life, for both boys and girls, and varies by race/ethnicity, and social class.

A third perspective, the social ecology model, suggests that negative community effects can be mediated by relationships between adolescents and their family, peers, and others in their communities (Denner et al. 2001). This perspective adds to the cultural adaptation framework by examining the intersection of social capital (community, parental, and kin support) and cultural norms. The social ecology model views social processes such as strong support networks, protective cultural norms, and family/community orientation as minimizers of the negative effects of poverty, adolescent pregnancy, and juvenile delinquency. Subsequently, this chapter is based on a social ecology perspective.

Review of Literature

Previous studies have noted a number of factors influencing adolescent pregnancy and motherhood, such as teenage sexual activity, school performance, family constellation (single female-headed households and level of parental supervision), quality of family relationships, socioeconomic factors, and fertility patterns of the communities in which the adolescents live (Sciarra and Ponterotto 1998). Much of the contemporary research on female adolescents has primarily focused on comparisons of white and African Americans, but less is known about Latina youth (Denner et al. 2001; Pesa and Matthews 2000; Erickson 1998; East 1998; Barratt and Roach 1996; Samuels, Stockdale, and Crase 1994). Some studies have identified social capital and cultural norms as important resources for adolescent mothers (Becerra and de Anda 1984; Passino and Whitman 1993; Koniak-Griffin, Lominska, and Brecht 1993; Barratt and Roach 1996; Hudson, Elek, and Campbell-Grossman 2000; Denner et al. 2001). Denner and colleagues (2001) found that communities with high social capital (parental and kin support, and other community resources) and strong protective cultural norms such as respect for the family tend to function as a safety factor for Latino youth.

Schaffer's (1996) research on the effects of ethnicity, generation, and socioeconomic status on the social networks of Mexican American and Anglo single mothers found that overall "Mexican American single mothers have larger and more internally cohesive support networking than do Anglos." She also found differences between first- and second-generation women: single mothers born in Mexico had fewer support networks than second-generation women. Unlike studies that found an increase in family networks by the third generation, Schaffer's results revealed that kin networks actually dropped for third-generation respondents. She suggests that by the third generation, Mexican American single mothers exhibit a "bicultural adaptation" pattern, whereby friends are added to existing familial networks.

Scholars such as Sciarra and Ponterotto (1998) note that interrelated cultural trends found among Latino families, such as the tendency to bequeath a preeminent role on motherhood, have close connections with and rely on the extended family and have more clearly defined roles for men and women. Acculturation is the process of learning, among other things, the behaviors (e.g., language and lifestyle) and beliefs and values of a host culture (Perez and Padilla 2000). Perez and Padilla (2000) studied acculturation across three generations of Latino adolescents and found that in a few generations the majority of Latino youth tend to increasingly move toward an American cultural framework. However, they note that across generations, adolescents continue to retain aspects of their Latino heritage, and this is especially true for familial values such as relying on family for emotional support.

The Strategy Research Corporation (1991) examined rates of acculturation among Latinos and found that Mexican Americans are experiencing a slow rate of acculturation with some regional and generational variations. Driscoll and colleagues' (2001) review of acculturation, as it relates to Latino reproductive health, notes that some of the research literature shows a link between acculturation and negative outcomes. They argue that we need more studies that examine which factors determine a youth's particular adaptation route. Examples of these factors include the influence of family attributes, the schooling experience, peers, and other environmental factors. Shapiro and Mangelsdorf (1994) examined the effects of social networks on mothers' adjustment to parenthood, among three different ethnic groups. They concluded that adaptation/adjustment to motherhood was positively influenced by family support for younger mothers, but not for older mothers. They speculated that some older mothers may perceive family support as interfering with their maternal role.

A study that investigated adolescent mothers' adjustment to parenting, self-esteem, social support, and perceptions of baby among fourteen- to twenty-year-old whites, Latinas, African Americans, Asian Americans, and Native Americans found that self-esteem was positively correlated to social support, adjustment to parenting, and contact with the baby's father (Samuels, Stockdale, and Crase 1994). Although the study did not discuss racial/ethnic differences, these findings suggest that supportive social networks lead to higher self-esteem and better adjustment to motherhood for adolescent women.

Sciarra and Ponterotto (1998) studied adolescent motherhood among low-income Latino families living in high-crime areas, with a focus on mother-daughter dyads. They found that adolescents' mothers played a crucial role in their daughters' pregnancies and motherhood, that relationships between the adolescents' mothers and fathers of the children were generally negative ones, and that adolescent mothers received support from their boyfriend's mothers and their families.

Method

Data Collection and Respondents

This study is based on in-depth interviews with thirty young Chicana mothers who gave birth between the ages of fourteen and eighteen. All of the adolescent mothers were from Riverside and San Bernardino Counties in Southern California. The first few respondents were contacted through two local community health services agencies through use of the snowball method. Each respondent completed a face-to-face semistructured, open-ended interview that lasted approximately 1.5 hours in one of two places: local community service agency that serves teen mothers and/or teen's home. The questions for the interview were designed to elicit both narrative and easily coded responses to sociodemographic data, perspectives on pregnancy, birthing experience, number and age of children, social support networks, self-esteem, acculturation, generation, and other questions related to the participants' social environment. All interviews were audio-taped and conducted in the preferred language of the respondent (English or Spanish). Twenty-five of the interviews were in English, while the remaining five were a combination of English and Spanish.

Informants ranged in age from fifteen to nineteen years old. Twenty-seven of the young mothers had one child, while three had two children. The children's ages ranged from one to four years old. When participants were asked about years of education completed, five said they had dropped out of high school, two said they had high school diplomas, one had a GED, two had one or two years of college, and twenty were still attending high school. Socioeconomic classification was based on the adolescent parent's level of education. Twenty of the adolescent mothers had parents from working-class backgrounds, while ten were middle class. Seven of the respondents lived with their mother and siblings, ten lived with both mother and father, and the remaining eight reported a combination of living arrangements (e.g., living with relatives or boyfriend and his family).

Elsa O. Valdez

Measures

Acculturation was measured in terms of cultural identification and orientation. Nine statements were adapted from Phinney's (1992) Multigroup Ethnic Identity Measure (MEIM), which includes statements about cultural pride, cultural practices, and cultural awareness. Respondents were read each of the nine statements, and their response was rated on a four-point scale ranging from strongly agree to strongly disagree. To assess instrumental support, respondents were first asked to identify family and/or nonfamily members who had been the most helpful in providing several types of assistance. Mothers were provided with a list of several types of instrumental support and asked to select from the following categories: child care, economic support, material items (e.g., clothing, diapers, toys, etc.), and transportation. Respondents were also asked which family or nonfamily member had given them the most emotional support. Adolescent mothers were categorized into three generational groups. Mothers born in Mexico were considered first generation (n = 4). Adolescents born in the United States but whose parents were born in Mexico were considered second generation (n = 15). Finally, Chicanas born in the United States whose parents were also born in the United States were labeled third generation (n = 11).

Adjustment to the mothering role was defined as the young mother's perception of the maternal role as either beneficial or burdensome. Participants were asked to describe their experience of being a mother, and what being a mother meant to them. They were prompted to be very specific and elaborate. Responses were then sorted into three categories: finds mothering role beneficial, finds mothering both beneficial and a burden, and finds mothering role a burden. To measure levels of self-esteem, subjects were administered a ten-item scale adapted from Coopersmith's Self-Esteem Scale (1965) and Rosenberg's Self-Esteem Scale (1965). Subjects were read each of the ten statements and had four options that ranged from strongly agree to strongly disagree.

Findings

Social Networks and Self-Esteem

The majority of respondents reported receiving high levels of instrumental support, such as help with child care, financial assistance, material items (e.g., clothing, diapers, etc.), and transportation (n = 20). When asked which person(s) had been the most useful to them in providing instrumental support, nineteen of the respondents identified their mother. The remaining participants said they received instrumental support from other family members such as a sister, brother, cousin, father, boyfriend, and grandmother. With respect to emotional support, thirteen of the teens reported that their mother filled this role, seven said that they did not get emotional support from their mother, nine said they received it from other family members, and one said she did not receive any support from family members. The data for self-esteem showed that the majority of young women exhibited high levels of self-esteem (n = 22) and eight had moderate levels.

Similar to other studies, these findings illustrate the Mexican American family's reliance on extended family networks (Schaffer 1996; Erickson 1998; Sciarra and Ponterotto 1998; Valdez 1996) and the significance of mothers' role in their daughters' pregnancies and motherhood (Sciarra and Ponterotto 1998). Additionally, it appears that there is a connection between self-esteem and social networks. Samuels, Stockdale, and Crase (1994) found a positive correlation between self-esteem and social networks, while Denner and colleagues (2001) concluded that communities with high social capital, such as parental–kin support, tended to have a protective influence on Latino youth. In this study as well, it is plausible that social networks mediate negative environmental factors as suggested by the social ecology model (Denner et al. 2001).

Acculturation, Generation, and Social Support

The findings indicate that overall, adolescent mothers experienced low (n = 16) to moderate (n = 13) levels of acculturation. Scores for respondents who experienced low acculturation ranged from 1.0 to 1.88. Of these mothers, two were first generation, seven were second, and seven were third. The scores for moderate levels of acculturation ranged from 2.0 to 2.77. For this group, two were first generation, six were second, and five were third. There was only one third-generation respondent with a high acculturation score of 3.5. Perez and Padilla's (2000) study found that although Latino adolescents become more acculturated across three generations, they retained familial aspects of their culture, such as emotional support. Other studies also found that acculturation and generation do not diminish familial values such as the importance of family and social support (Erickson 1998). It appears that in this sample there is a positive interaction between social capital and cultural norms, and that acculturation has not decreased the importance of family support among second- and third-generation Chicana mothers. Driscoll and colleagues (2001) maintain that acculturation is detrimental to Latino youth, and that gradual acculturation is inevitable. These young mothers have found that it is advantageous to retain familial aspects of culture and reliance on extended family networks, which in turn helps offset some of the negative aspects of acculturation.

Perceptions of Motherhood

Adolescent mothers' perceptions of motherhood were overall positive. Nineteen respondents said that they felt motherhood was beneficial, six said it was both beneficial and a burden, and five perceived it in negative terms.

Perceptions of Motherhood as Beneficial

Three trends emerged from responses of mothers who viewed parenthood as positive. First, they enjoyed being a mother. Marilyn, a seventeen-year-old mother with a two-year-old daughter, said, "I was excited when I was pregnant with her, knowing she was going to be born and I could finally hold her in my arms. I really enjoy being a mom, feeding her, and caring for her." Another theme was how rewarding it was to be a parent. One mother said that "it's hard sometimes, but to see a child grow and develop is the most rewarding job a person can have." Belin commented, "It's something so special and rewarding that I get emotional just talking about it. To think that I could love someone so much is hard to explain." A third trend was how they had made adjustments with respect to behavior and goals. Corrine commented, "I am more patient now, which I wasn't before he came along. I think more about the future and how I can be a better person." Vanessa said she planned to stay in school because "now I have to think about the future. Before it wasn't that important to finish high school. Now that I'm responsible for my son, I need to get a good education so that I can get ahead for both of us." For the most part, the majority of the subjects who reported viewing motherhood as beneficial also said that their mother was the most helpful person and provided both instrumental and emotional support. They also tended to have high levels of self-esteem.

Mixed Perceptions of Motherhood

Several common themes emerged from mothers who said that being a mother was both negative and positive. First, they mentioned what a huge responsibility it was to be a mother. Two of the respondents described how scared and anxious they felt because now they were responsible for a new life. A second theme was that although it was stressful at times, there were a lot of rewards. Fifteen-year-old Blanca reflected that "I didn't know what to expect and at first it didn't feel like he was mine. Then I started to get to know him better and it was less confusing and more enjoyable."

Perceptions of Motherhood as Burdensome

Adolescents with negative perceptions stressed the amount of work that was involved in caring for a child and lack of support from the child's father; for example, lack of sleep, irritable temperament, difficult babies, feelings of being overwhelmed, and having problems with the baby's father and/or his family. One nineteen-year-old participant found motherhood to be very difficult and described what it's like to be the mother of a four-year-old. While Veronica had a good support system, two years of college, and a moderate level of self-esteem, she had no contact with her daughter's father.

> I go through times when I don't want to be a mom. I thought about adoption. It also made a difference because her father did not want to have anything to do with us. If he was in the picture and was supportive it might be different. I'm trying to bond more with my daughter . . . I think it's getting better. I didn't want her at first because I wanted to go out. I wanted to give her to someone close to the family, like my aunt. I still feel guilty because I felt that way. She was difficult when she was born. She had colic all the time. After the colic there was a lot of whining and crying. There were times when I couldn't sleep and I was so tired. Things have gotten a little bit better. I'm a little bit closer to my daughter than I was before.

Shirley, a seventeen-year-old who had a one-year-old child, commented that "it's really hard, I have my family, but to me it's not really enough. If I could go back I would change everything." She lived with her aunt and lamented the fact that her child's father did not give her financial support, although he babysat occasionally. Before she lived with her aunt, Shirley lived in a series of foster homes. Two other teen mothers emphasized the difficulty of juggling various roles at one time. Another teen mother, seventeen-year-old Diana who reported high self-esteem but only occasional visits from the baby's father, commented, "It's hard to do everything all at once—going to school, having a boyfriend, trying to be responsible. It's easy to take care of my son, what's really hard are the problems with family and all of that." Seventeen-year-old Marisol, who saw the baby's father once a month, complained about not getting any emotional or financial support and the stresses of being a single mother,

> It's hard, I like to sleep late but my son doesn't. He wakes up every two hours and wants milk, so I have to get up. I can't do my chores around the house because he cries. When he was born I used to work, go to school, and go to night school. I stay home more because I was afraid he would think grandma was mom.

The absence of contact with the baby's father or support from him was also a common theme among the other respondents who perceived parenthood as burdensome.

Discussion and Recommendations

Overall, these findings are supported by Schaffer's (1996) study, which found that Mexican American single mothers tend to have higher social support networks than other groups, and Sciarra and Ponterotto (1998), who maintain that Latina mothers play a significant role in their adolescent daughters' pregnancies and parenthood. Moreover, Samuels, Stockdale, and Crase's (1994) study of Latina and other racial/ethnic adolescent mothers found a positive relationship between adjustment to parenting, self-esteem, social support, and perceptions of child. Finally, studies examining the acculturation of Latinos/Chicanos show that while Latino/Mexican Americans are slowly acculturating, they tend to retain aspects of their heritage such as familial support (Perez and Padilla 2000; Strategy Research Corporation 1991). However, this study differs from Schaffer's (1996) study, which found that kin networks tend to decrease for third-generation Mexican American single mothers. For these young mothers who are primarily second and third generation, family networks continue to be an important source of instrumental and emotional support. In short, it appears that high levels of social support/social capital and retention of cultural norms positively affect self-esteem, as well as adolescent mothers' perceptions of parenthood. Additionally, acculturation and generation do not appear to diminish the importance of *la familia* for these Chicana mothers.

What are some implications that we need to consider? First, we need to redefine the so-called American value system to reflect the diverse cultural norms that exist. A good place to start is with the educational system, where "forced assimilation" of minority and immigrant groups tends to be a primary goal. In general, Mexican and Mexican American families emphasize values such as familism, bilingualism, and extended family ties, which are often viewed as detrimental to successful integration of immigrant groups. We are a multicultural society composed of families from around the world. Southern California, in particular, has a high number of Mexican-origin families. Numerous studies show that social capital, nonacculturation, and retention of cultural norms benefit young mothers, especially minority adolescents.

Consequently, if programs servicing young Chicana/Latina mothers are to be more effective, it is essential that intervention practices be based on a social ecology model. Familism, cultural norms, and nonacculturation should be considered important minimizers of the negative effects of adolescent parenting. As noted by Erickson, "Cultural and social context combine to support early childbearing among Latina adolescents . . . the current types of intervention programs—targeted to individual behavior change, based on middle-class life script norms, institution based and short term—cannot be expected to have more than a limited impact on childbearing" (1998, 163).

Second, most studies of female adolescents tend to focus on comparative analyses of whites and African Americans. We need to conduct both quantitative and qualitative studies that include comparisons of Latina subgroups and racial/ethnic comparisons that include Chicana/Latina adolescents. A third related recommendation is the need for establishing a national organization and database with the long-term objective of addressing the multifaceted issues of teenage pregnancy, early motherhood, and other Latino youth issues, such as health and education. On a state-regional level, it would be beneficial to develop a research/advocacy center that primarily focuses on Mexican American/Latino youth. Since the Chicano/Latino population is very young, it is imperative that we pay more attention to this segment of the population. While there are agencies and organizations that address these concerns (e.g., National Council of La Raza, National Campaign to Prevent Teen Pregnancy, and the Alan Guttmacher Institute), there is limited funding available and few resources to conduct research that is proactive rather than reactive. It is essential that funding and future research initiatives be proportionate to the needs of the expanding Chicano/Latino population, as well as other minority groups.

References

Barratt, Marguerite S., and Mary A. Roach. 1996. "Adjustment to Motherhood by Single Adolescents." *Family Relations* 45, no. 2: 209–16.

Becerra, Rosina M., and Diana de Anda. 1984. "Pregnancy and Motherhood among Mexican American Adolescents." *Health and Social Work* 9, no. 2: 106–23.

Coopersmith, Stanley. 1967. *The Antecedents of Self-Esteem.* San Francisco: Freeman, 1967.

Denner, Jill, Douglas Kirby, Karin Coyle, and Claire Brindis. 2001. "The Protective Role of Social Capital and Cultural Norms in Latino Communities: A Study of Adolescent Births." *Hispanic Journal of Behavioral Sciences* 23, no. 1: 3–16.

Driscoll, Anne I., Antonia M. Biggs, Claire D. Brindis, and Ekua Yankah. 2001. "Adolescent Latino Reproductive Health: A Review of the Literature." *Hispanic Journal of Behavioral Sciences* 23, no. 3: 255–327.

East, Patricia L. 1998. "Racial and Ethnic Differences in Girls' Sexual, Marital, and Birth Expectations." *Journal of Marriage and the Family* 60, no. 1: 150–63.

Erickson, Pamela I. 1998. *Latina Adolescent Childbearing in East Los Angeles.* Austin, TX: University of Texas Press, 1998.

Franklin, Donna L. 1992. "Early Childbearing Patterns Among African Americans: A Socio-Historical Perspective." In *Early Parenthood and Coming of Age in the 1990s,* ed. Margaret K. Rosenheim and Mark F. Testa, 55–70. Piscataway, NJ: Rutgers University Press.

Hamburg, Beatrix A., and Sandra Lee Dixon. 1992. "Adolescent Pregnancy and Parenthood." In *Early Parenthood and Coming of Age in the 1990s*, ed. Margaret K. Rosenheim and Mark F. Testa, 17–33. Piscataway, NJ: Rutgers University Press.

Hudson, Diane Brage, Susan M. Elek, and Christie Campbell-Grossman. 2000. "Depression, Self-Esteem, Loneliness, and Social Support among Adolescent Mothers Participating in the New Parent's Project." *Adolescence* 35: 445–66.

Kaplan, Elaine Bell. 1997. *Not Our Kind of Girl*. Berkeley: University of California Press.

Keefe, Susan E., and Amado M. Padilla. 1987. *Chicano Ethnicity*. Albuquerque: University of New Mexico Press.

Koniak-Griffin, Deborah, Susan Lominska, and Mary-Lynn Brecht. 1993. "Social Support during Pregnancy: A Comparison of Three Ethnic Groups." *Journal of Adolescence* 16, no. 1: 43–56.

Ladner, Joyce A. 1972. *Tomorrow's Tomorrow*. New York: Anchor.

National Campaign to Prevent Teen Pregnancy. 2001. *Teen Sexual Activity, Pregnancy, and Childbearing among Latinos in the United States*. Teenpregnancy.org. www.teenpregnancy.org/resources/data/genlfact.asp (August 8, 2002).

Passino, Anne W., and Thomas L. Whitman. 1993. "Personal Adjustment during Pregnancy and Adolescent Parenting." *Adolescence* 28: 97–122.

Perez, Sonia M., et al. 2001. "Beyond the Census: Hispanics and an American Agenda." *National Council of La Raza*. www.nclr.org (August 8, 2002).

Perez, William, and Amado M. Padilla. 2000. "Cultural Orientation across Three Generations of Hispanic Adolescents." *Hispanic Journal of Behavioral Sciences* 22, no. 3: 390–99.

Pesa, Jacqueline A., and Jeff Matthews. 2000. "The Relationship between Barriers to Birth Control Use and Actual Birth Control Use among Mexican-American Adolescents." *Adolescence* 35: 695–708.

Phinney, Jean S. 1992. "The Multigroup Ethnic Identity Measure: A New Scale for Use with Diverse Populations." *Journal of Adolescent Research* 7, no. 2: 156–76.

Rosenberg, Morris. 1965. *Society and the Adolescent Self-Image*. Princeton, NJ: Princeton University Press.

Saenz, Rogelio, Maria C. Morales, and Janie Filoteo. 2004. "The Demography of Mexicans in the United States." In *Chicanas and Chicanos in Contemporary Society*, ed. Roberto M. De Anda, chap. 1. Lanham, Md.: Rowman & Littlefield.

Samuels, Valerie Jarvis, Dahlia F. Stockdale, and Sedahlia Jasper Crase. 1994. "Adolescent Mothers' Adjustment to Parenting." *Journal of Adolescence* 17, no. 5: 427–43.

Schaffer, Diane M. 1996. "Mexican American and Anglo Single Mothers: The Influence of Ethnicity, Generation, and Socioeconomic Status on Social Support Network." *Hispanic Journal of Behavioral Sciences* 18, no. 1: 74–87.

Sciarra, Daniel T., and Joseph G. Ponterotto. 1998. "Adolescent Motherhood among Low Income Urban Hispanics: Familial Considerations of Mother-Daughter Dyads." *Qualitative Health Research* 8, no. 6: 751–76.

Shapiro, Janet R., and Sarah C. Mangelsdorf. 1994. "The Determinants of Parenting Competence in Adolescent Mothers." *Journal of Youth and Adolescence* 23: 621–41.

Stack, Carol. 1974. *All Our Kin.* New York: Harper & Row.

Staples, Robert. 1985. "Changes in Black Family Structure: The Conflict between Family Ideology and Structural Conditions." *Journal of Marriage and the Family* 47 (1985): 1005–12.

Strategy Research Corporation. 1991. *U.S. Hispanic Market,* 109–20.

Valdez, Elsa O. 1996. "Chicano Families and Urban Poverty: Familial Strategies of Cultural Retention." In *Chicanas and Chicanos in Contemporary Society,* ed. Roberto M. De Anda, 63–74. Needham Heights, MA: Allyn & Bacon.

7

"Let's Unite So That Our Children Are Better Off Than Us": Mexican American/Mexican Immigrant Women Organizing for Bilingual Education

Gilda Laura Ochoa

IN 1996 A LOS ANGELES–AREA SCHOOL DISTRICT considered abolishing bilingual education and establishing an English-only policy, and a group of primarily working-class Mexican American and Mexican immigrant women responded by forming Parents for Quality Education.[1] Determined to maintain bilingual education, members of Parents for Quality Education, along with another parent group, organized a signature campaign and a joint demonstration/candle light vigil. By applying pressure to the school district, both parent groups ensured the continuation of bilingual education until the passage of California State Proposition 227 in 1998, which resulted in its elimination. They also demonstrated the power of grassroots organizing.

Such examples of political activism on the part of women of Mexican descent are not new. However, until fairly recently, the sociological scholarship on this topic has been scant.[2] The literature on multiple forms of activism has been limited by narrow conceptualizations of race/ethnic relations, gender and race, and political activism.[3] Until the 1970s, much of the scholarship on race/ethnic relations was framed in a black/white dichotomy, largely excluding the experiences of Latinas/Latinos as well as Native Americans and Asian Americans (Martínez 1998). Furthermore, until the 1980s, it was common for scholars to conceive of gender and race as distinct categories, as opposed to analyzing the ways that gender, race/ethnicity, and class are interconnected and simultaneous. Such "either/or dichotomous thinking" often resulted in work that focused on either gender oppression and the experiences of white women or on racial oppression and the experiences of men of color, marginalizing the experiences of Latinas and other women of color (Collins 1990; Espiritu 1997). Likewise, traditional conceptions of activism have been defined narrowly (Hardy-Fanta 1993; Cohen, Jones, and Tronto 1997). There has been a tendency to equate political activity with elections, strikes, and demonstrations that occur in official and public arenas such as unions and political parties, overlooking the less structured and more individual forms of resistance that women may engage in within their homes and communities and the ways that racism, sexism, and poverty may exclude Latinas from organized political movements (Collins 1990; Soldatenko 1991; Ochoa 1999).

More recently, an emerging body of sociological scholarship has analyzed the multiple forms of activism, resistance, and politics among Latinas, including resistance undertaken in homes, work sites, churches, and communities (see Zavella 1987; Pardo 1991; Hardy-Fanta 1993; Méndez-Negrete 1999; Ochoa 1999). As well as broadening the conceptualization of activism, this scholarship considers how organizing activities are influenced by race/ethnicity, class, and gender, revealing how women's activism is often linked to family concerns and community networks (Hardy-Fanta 1993; Naples 1998; Pardo 1998).

By centering the activities of the women of Parents for Quality Education, this chapter further illustrates how organizing and activist strategies often emerge from and are grounded in the social positions of its members. As a largely working-class, Mexican-descent, and female-led group, Parents for Quality Education advanced ideologies and engaged in practices that were intimately connected to the social locations of its organizers as bilingual women and mothers of Mexican descent. Through participatory and inclusive politics, the group drew on members' community networks and employed gender-conscious activities to integrate women and families in their fight for bilingual education. Aware of the multiple responsibilities of women, the organizers combined gendered and raced expectations of reproductive labor with political activism. This reproductive labor includes, but is not limited to, buying and preparing food, providing emotional support, care, nurturance, and socialization for family members, maintaining and transmitting culture, and establishing family and community connections (Dill 1994, 167; Baca Zinn 1994, 308; Glenn 1992, 1). Through their organizing activities, Parents for Quality Education challenged dominant ideologies and structures by confronting the racial/ethnic hierarchy that favors English over Spanish, redefining the relationship between working-class parents and school officials, and reconceptualizing traditional gender roles and notions of mothering. An analysis of this parent group contributes to our understanding of how Latinas, within their homes, communities, and schools, act in politicized and transformative ways as they work for the good of their children and their communities.

Research Setting and Methods

Participants of Parents for Quality Education reside in the predominately working-class Latina/Latino communities of La Puente and Valinda in the Los Angeles County. Their children attend schools in the Hacienda–La Puente Unified School District (HLPUSD), one of the largest districts in the East San Gabriel Valley.[4] In 1996, at the time of the group's formation, the district's thirty-five campuses had a K-12 enrollment of over 22,000 students, and nearly half of the La Puente-area students entering kindergarten did not speak English (*San Gabriel Valley Tribune*, June 24, 1996). Given the racial/ethnic demographics of the communities, it is not surprising that La Puente-area residents mobilized when school board members considered a proposal to eliminate bilingual education.

During this period, I was interviewing Mexican Americans and Mexican immigrants in La Puente on intraethnic relations.[5] I was attending city council meetings, community meetings, and school-based meetings. Through my attendance at school district meetings, I met the primary organizers of Parents for Quality Education, Raquel Heinrich, a Mexican immigrant woman, and Irene Renteria-Salazar, a Mexican American woman. I completed a series of in-depth, semistructured, open-ended interviews with them on their experiences, organizing philosophies, and activities.[6] After these interviews, the organizers invited me to their group activities, where I was introduced to and subsequently conducted participant observations and informal interviews with the eight group members who were most actively involved. The interviews focused on the factors leading to the formation of Parents for Quality Education and the group's organizing activities. Interviews were audio-taped, fully transcribed, and subsequently analyzed for recurring themes and patterns. The quotes appearing in this chapter are verbatim from the transcripts.

Organizing Parents for Quality Education

Formed in response to the school district proposal to eliminate bilingual education, Parents for Quality Education was largely shaped by its organizers, Raquel Heinrich and Irene Renteria-Salazar. They employed a gender-aware approach that linked their organizing philosophies and strategies to their own experiences and social positions. Both women are strong supporters of bilingual education. Raquel Heinrich, who migrated at the age of eighteen from a small town in Mexico in 1975, believes that raising bilingual children helps ensure that they are proud of their racial/ethnic background and that they have multiple life and career opportunities. Born in the historically Mexican-origin community of East Los Angeles to immigrant parents, Irene Renteria-Salazar learned to speak Spanish first. She draws on her early educational experiences of feeling excluded in classes and by English-speaking students to argue that bilingual education fosters high self-esteem and positive intraethnic relations between Mexican Americans and Mexican immigrants.

The organizers' support for bilingual education led them to participate in various school and district committees on bilingual education. Based on these experiences in the schools and as workingwomen with elementary-age children, as they formed their organization, they drew on their positive exchanges with school officials to advocate working collaboratively and inclusively. They were especially attuned to women's multiple gender role responsibilities, and they equated raising bilingual children with "good mothering."

Working Collectively and Inclusively

A key philosophy in Parents for Quality Education was working collectively to maintain bilingual education and ensure that all children in the school district obtain quality education. This emphasis stemmed from the organizers' belief that every member of the community has an important role in ensuring community well-being and that everyone benefits from the education of children. Raquel Heinrich explained the group's underlying ideology:

> In this community, we are always going to have children. We are always going to have schools, and we are always going to have teachers and parents. None of these entities can function without the other.

Raquel and Irene stressed collaboration on multiple levels. According to the group's mission statement, one level involved developing "a partnership" between teachers and parents by participating in classrooms and at school events. Another level entailed providing advice and assistance to school and district officials as well as attending school board meetings. Raquel elaborated on these group goals:

> The goal is to develop an organization that will be able to be there to work hand and hand with the district, with the administration, with the teachers, with the principals, and with the board that is going to say, "Okay, which way is the right way to approach education? What programs are good? How can we help on something that is going to benefit the community and the children?"

By defining their relationship with school officials as a partnership, Parents for Quality Education moved beyond the expectations that some teachers and administrators have of working-class parents. As Shannon explained, "Teachers . . . generally want parents to assume the role of audience" in their relationship with schools (1996, 72). In this role, parent participation may be encouraged only when it is structured by school personnel in such events as back-to-school night, teacher-parent conferences, or school-affiliated organizations as in Parent–Teacher Associations (Shannon 1996; Shannon and Latimer 1996). In addition to working within this framework, Parents for Quality Education advocated asking questions and providing recommendations to school officials, an approach that conceptualized parents as critical contributors to ensuring that schools serve the interests of communities.

Shared experiences of inequality and discrimination faced by many Mexican-origin women may foster their larger struggle for what Raquel described as "something that is going to benefit the community." As others have also demonstrated, while women of color's community involvement may originate in a concern for their own children, they often conceptualize their struggle as something important for uplifting the entire race (Collins 1990; Naples 1998; Pardo 1998). Instead of being an institution that reinforces capitalism's emphasis on individualistic concerns, motherhood, as defined by such women, can provide a basis for community-building, activism, and social justice.

The organizers characterized their group as inclusive. They argued that school district decisions affected not only La Puente students and parents but also families and businesses in the unincorporated areas of Valinda and Hacienda Heights. Parents for Quality Education believed that their name alone, which did not single out one particular city or region, demonstrated their inclusivity. As Raquel described, the group's intent paralleled the rationale behind the group's name:

> We have to develop an organization that is going to maintain and sustain the quality education for our child, regardless of which community we are. We're not isolating anybody. We don't want to say, "This is only for English-speaking or only for La Puente parents, or only for Valinda parents because the unified school district covers four [areas]."[7]

Parents for Quality Education sought various ways to "work hand and hand" to include community members in their group activities. They integrated elected officials, Catholic churches, and business owners by approaching them with opportunities to provide assistance. For example, local business donated food and drinks for some of the group's events, and several politicians wrote letters to the school board indicating their support of bilingual education while others attended meetings or sent representatives.

Parents for Quality Education's emphasis on collectivity and inclusion may stem from the organizers' positions as women. Researchers have found that in comparison to their male counterparts, women leaders of Mexican descent tend to stress working collaboratively and engaging people with common interests (Hardy-Fanta 1993; Méndez-Negrete 1999). This emphasis was made explicit in Parents for Quality Education's organizing strategies as they sought ways to facilitate the participation of women.

Paying Attention to Gender, Race/Ethnicity, and Class

Raquel and Irene were strategic in how they organized group meetings and events. Meetings were planned to best accommodate the competing demands that they as well as most of the group members experienced as working women with families. Raquel emphasized the importance of considering people's multiple commitments:

> I know more or less how to [organize an event], and I can probably get it done, but I know that doing it alone is not possible not just because I have two kids but because I see the other parents who are [also] working. We are going to have to mold [meetings and events] around their schedules. We are going to have to mold [activities] around the ones that do have a lot of time, but without burning them out either.

Aware of people's time constraints and many responsibilities, the group tended to organize meetings at Raquel's home, a convenient place known by many families in her community because of the intimate relationships that she has developed with her Latina/Latino neighbors. During these meetings, families were invited and, to reduce the amount of strain on women, the organizers often provided food and drinks. Raquel explained the rationale underlying this organizing approach:

> So I don't burn out myself or anybody else, we have to [organize] around our family needs. I like to include the family. The [meeting] on Sunday, [we] thought, Let's make it a Father's Day event.

As well as designing family-friendly group meetings, they characterized other activities as "family events." For example, following a large meeting at a local Catholic church attended by over seventy-five people, the group formed a committee that would gather signatures in support of bilingual education and invite people to a protest and vigil that they were organizing. As part of this committee, a family volunteered to disseminate information outside of Catholic churches. Raquel described how the family arrived at the church early Sunday morning and worked together to educate the community:

They showed up, not only husband and wife. They were carrying a baby, and they had a stroller with a two-year-old, and their ten-year-old was passing out flyers with them. So, they took turns signing people up, passing the flyers out, inviting [people] to the meetings, and signing the petition [in favor of bilingual education]. So, I was very proud to see that it was a family event.

Many of the activists were motivated by concern for their children and hope for their future. They also located their involvement in their own experiences of prejudice and discrimination. Writing in the group's first newsletter, Norma Mendoza described why she became interested in the group's activities:

I, as a mother, am very happy to [give] a little bit of my time to defend the rights of my children. I want their future to be better than mine . . . Bilingual education is very important for me because I want my children to be able to defend themselves, so that they don't go through what most of us go through because we are not able to defend ourselves. [English speakers] have [humiliated] me, but I will do everything I can to make sure that my children are not humiliated. Let's unite so that our children are better off than us.

For Norma Mendoza, and other members of Parents for Quality Education, fighting to maintain bilingual education is one way that she is working to ensure that Latina/Latino children will have the skills to defend themselves against the humiliation encountered by their parents. Norma's political activism emerged from her experiences of discrimination as a Mexican immigrant working-class woman and her position as a mother, defending "the rights of [her] children."

Similarly, Irene discussed the significance of gender in the community activism of Latinas by reflecting on her experiences and the interdependence between the role of Latinas as reproductive laborers and their participation in school affairs:

In the Hispanic community or the Hispanic family . . . women are the ones that take care of the education of the children, so I think that's the reason why we have more women involved in [Parents for Quality Education] even though we had a lot of men [demonstrating at the school board], but they're not willing to give their time to come to meetings . . . Once you tell [the men] exactly what's going to be done, they'll be there in the front, but they won't be always at the planning end. "No, that's women stuff." It's almost like . . . in the house . . . my dad used to be the same way. He never would go to any meetings, but if you told him he would have to be there at a certain time to do something, then he'd be there, but Mom always took care of all the stuff that has to do with education.

Both Irene and Raquel attributed women's and men's activism in Parents for Quality Education to their respective gender roles. They equated the division of labor within their organization to the division of labor in the household. Attributing the mostly female involvement in the daily running of the group's activities to women's gender role expectations, Irene expected men to support their activities and appear when requested at specific events. As evidenced by her quote, Irene was acutely aware that while men may not be "willing to give their time" for meetings, at such public events as demonstrations "they'll be there in the front."

Raquel also highlighted the significance of men's support in their activities and their occasional but nonetheless important participation in key events such as their involvement in a pro-bilingual education demonstration organized at the district office before a school board study session on bilingual education:

> [Our meeting on Father's Day] was the first time that I saw the video, the one my husband is putting together [on the demonstration before the study session]. [Through the video], it was the first time that I saw the magnitude on the part of the men on the picket line. [Seeing the large number of men] was what I was very proud of. So, regardless of who takes part in the event planning, as long as the men are there to support what we are doing, I am happy with it.

The extensive participation of men that Raquel observed in the video may be a visual reflection of Irene's point that men tended to "be [out] there in the front" while the women were actually the ones planning and organizing the daily activities from behind. At this demonstration, it may have been the men who were physically near the front of the protesters. Regardless of what might account for the "magnitude on the part of the men on the picket line," both Irene and Raquel were pleased with the men's support. By defining men's responsibilities as "supporters" in the struggle for bilingual education, the organizers challenged dominant conceptions of political activism where men are usually conceived as the leaders and women are typically cast in auxiliary roles.

The gender differences in levels and types of participation described by Irene and Raquel may be attributed to men and women's differing social roles as well as to structural barriers. Nine out of the ten people who consistently attended group meetings were women. Women's involvement in the group's activities was facilitated by the inclusion of families, as in the meeting on Father's Day, as well as the close relationships Raquel has developed with her neighbors.

Overall, this higher level of women's participation in the everyday activities of Parents for Quality Education supports the existing literature that illustrates the connection, especially for women of color, between motherhood, a concern for one's children, and community involvement (Collins 1990;

Hardy-Fanta 1993; Naples 1998; Pardo 1998). These connections often result from women's gender role activities that may include such reproductive labor as taking children to school and to church, volunteering in neighborhood organizations, and nurturing and watching community children. As a result of these activities, women may interact with community members in ways that men may not. In their qualitative study of race relations in Philadelphia, Goode and Schneider observe that women often do the "social work of neighboring" because men's contact with the community may be limited by work outside of the neighborhood (1994, 148). Lamphere notes that women, as opposed to men, often cross boundaries, make connections, and create coalitions with immigrants (1992, 28). Similarly, as Hardy-Fanta's research on political activism demonstrates, in comparison to their male counterparts, Latinas may be more inclined to combine everyday relationships with political activism (1993, 29). It is precisely these gendered activities that may position women in critical roles to build coalitions and to impact change locally.

Supporting Bilingualism as an Example of "Good Mothering"

Parents for Quality Education underscored the psychological, social, and economic benefits of being Spanish-English bilingual. They believe that raising bilingual children is one way that they can enhance their children's life chances. Irene's reflections on bilingual education are illustrative:

> I think that bilingual education boosts the morale of the child, the confidence level. It also makes them be more of an extrovert . . . [Bilingual education] opens doors to jobs, to help other people that are not English-speaking . . . I think it is wonderful that we are allowing the opportunity to teach our children in bilingual instruction. They learn and master their language, and eventually the English will be picked up.

Raquel elaborated:

> The importance of [bilingual education] has a lot to do with making sure the child will have a career that has no limits. Having a child be fluently bilingual will not only open the doors in this country, but anywhere else . . . Every child should be able to have two languages, and what better language than Spanish which is one of the most spoken [languages] around the world . . . [Being bilingual] helped me, and it opened many doors, and now, more than ever, I am the most proud to be bilingual. So, I can have that pride and know that my children, when they become bilingual, they are going to feel proud of themselves.

Personally experiencing the benefits and seeing the positive implications of bilingualism for their children, both Raquel and Irene equate effective mothering or parenting with raising bilingual children and supporting bilingual education. This sentiment was apparent in Raquel's attempts to persuade a fellow parent to sign a petition in favor of bilingual education.

> When I was collecting signatures [in support of bilingual education], I went inside the classroom, and I asked a parent aide, who was assisting preschoolers, whether she would sign the petition. She said, "No, I don't believe in bilingual education." She spoke perfect English . . . I asked her, "Where is your husband from?" She said he was from Mexico. I said, "Your child will not be bilingual?" She said, "Of course not." I said, "Well, guess what? You are closing to your kid an extra door. That is what you are doing. All of his friends, look around you, all of the kids are Latino. So is your kid, whether you like it or not—he is Latino. You are closing a door on him because what you are doing is putting him in a position that if he wants to go to Mexico, Central America, anywhere in the world . . . By the year 2000, Spanish is going to be the language of the world, and you are closing the door on him. So, if you want to do that to your kid." She said, "Okay, where do I sign?"

Raquel's argument to a potential supporter of bilingual education parallels the linkages that she and Irene make between motherhood, a concern for one's children, and community participation. In this case, Raquel equated not teaching one's children Spanish and not supporting bilingual education to "poor mothering." By stating that the woman is "closing the door [on her child]" because he does not speak Spanish, Raquel called into question how a mother could knowingly limit her child's opportunities. The implication is that since Raquel is advocating for the needs of Latina/Latino children and the community by fighting to maintain bilingual education, she is a "good mother" (see Naples 1998, 113–14). When placed in a historical and contemporary context where learning and speaking English as quickly as possible have been the prevailing expectation, Raquel's conceptualization of "good mothering" directly challenged dominant perceptions that speaking Spanish to one's children makes one an "unfit parent" and that it hinders the advancement of children.[8]

Conclusion

Parents for Quality Education is one example of the long history of organizing on the part of the Mexican-origin community and the role of women in such organizing attempts. An examination of the intragroup dynamics and processes allows for a greater understanding of the ways that race/ethnicity, class, and gender influence organizers' philosophies and strategies. Using terminology such as developing a "partnership," "working hand and hand," and employing an "open door policy," the organizers emphasized collaboration for the good of the children and the community. Centering education, they maintained a narrowly defined focus to organize parents, an approach believed to be more inclusive because it brings together people who may agree on only one issue and not necessarily multiple ones (Friedman and McAdam 1992). They advocated improving the education of children and parents through involvement in multiple arenas. The group's mission statement encouraged its members to "participate in the daily activities of their children's education, not only at school and throughout [their] communities, but also at home."

Parents for Quality Education's political activism in regard to education confirms existing scholarship illustrating that women of color often mobilize around issues central to their daily lives (Hardy-Fanta 1993). Characterizing their struggle for quality education as part of their gendered responsibilities as mothers, Raquel and Irene illustrate how it was precisely their familial responsibilities as Latinas that fostered their political activism (see Hardy-Fanta 1993).

An initial examination of the group's philosophies and strategies might lead one to conclude that Parents for Quality Education's strategies and activities were conservative or not as radical as the activities of other groups—activities undertaken by mothers with a concern for their families or as parents working within the institutional confines of schools by assisting administrators and teachers. However, as others have also documented, women of color often engage in "revolutionary acts" in their roles as mothers as they work for the greater good of the community—for racial uplift and for group survival (Collins 1990; Pardo 1998; Krauss 1998; Naples 1998, 112). For Raquel and Irene, this "activist mothering" involved challenging "English only" for their own children and for the larger Latina/Latino community (see Naples 1998). Linking their political activism to their role as mothers, they reconceptualized narrowly defined gender role expectations.

Raquel and Irene were leaders who defined the role of their husbands and other men as "supporters." They drew on community resources and applied pressure to largely male business owners and politicians to provide assistance. By defining men's responsibilities as "supporters," they challenged dominant conceptions of political activism where men are usually conceived as the organizers and women are typically cast in auxiliary roles.

Parents for Quality Education also transcended the role of passive-parents often expected of school officials. By raising questions, giving advice, and characterizing their relationship with school officials as a partnership, they confronted practices that may limit parental activism in schools. They directly challenged myths about Mexican-descent parents as submissive, uninterested, apathetic, or nonpolitical regarding their children's education. In all of these ways, the organizers and participants of Parents for Quality Education acted in politicized and transformative ways. These findings confirm the ways that women are expanding traditional conceptions of mothering, politics, and activism.

Notes

1. A proposal sought to eliminate all Spanish reading and stop training teachers for bilingual credentials.

2. Aware of the politics of racial/ethnic labels, I use the term "Mexican American" when referring to Mexicans born in the United States and "Mexican immigrant" when referring to people born in Mexico and currently living in the United States. Both groups are referred to collectively as individuals of Mexican descent or members of the Mexican-origin community. The panethnic term "Latino/Latina" is used when referring to more than one Latina/Latino ethnic group.

3. I use the term "race/ethnicity" to capture the experiences of individuals of Mexican descent in the United States. I do not use it to conflate race and ethnicity but instead to acknowledge that they are two interrelated systems that have worked in ways that shape the life chances and experiences of the Mexican-origin community. While Mexican Americans and Mexican immigrants are usually discussed as an ethnic group that shares cultural characteristics, in the United States they have been racialized and socially constructed as distinct from whites both racially and ethnically.

4. The majority of students from this school district live in La Puente and Hacienda Heights. As I have described elsewhere, La Puente and Hacienda Heights differ by class and race/ethnicity (see Ochoa forthcoming). Hacienda Heights is more racially/ethnically diverse and middle class. Valinda, an unincorporated area of Los Angeles, is just south of La Puente. The racial/ethnic and class composition of Valinda resembles the demographic profile of the city of La Puente, and students from Valinda attend schools with La Puente students. I use the term "La Puente area" to refer to both Valinda and La Puente.

5. As part of this larger study, I conducted seventy open-ended interviews and twenty informal interviews with residents, institutional representatives, and community organizers between 1994 and 1996 and again in 2000 (see Ochoa forthcoming).

6. While most of the group's participants did not mind if their names were used, to be systematic and to respect the privacy of their family members, respondents' names have been changed. The name changes were selected to approximate the racial/ethnic ancestry of the actual names.

7. While the majority of students in the Hacienda–La Puente Unified School District reside in these two areas, there are some students from Valinda and Rowland Heights whose neighborhood schools are located within the HLPUSD.

8. This perception was made explicit on August 28, 1995, when a state district judge threatened a Texas mother with losing custody of her five-year-old child if she did not speak to her in English (Gonzalez 2000, 206). For some, the belief that speaking Span-

ish hinders advancement underlies their support for the English-only movement and the elimination of bilingual education.

References

Baca Zinn, Maxine. 1994. "Feminist Rethinking from Racial-Ethnic Families." In *Women of Color in U.S. Society*, ed. Maxine Baca Zinn and Bonnie Thornton Dill, 303–14. Philadelphia: Temple University Press.

Cohen, Cathy J., Kathleen B. Jones, and Joan C. Tronto. 1997. "Introduction: Women Transforming U.S. Politics: Sites of Power/Resistance. In *Women Transforming Politics: An Alternative Reader*, ed. Cathy J. Cohen, Kathleen B. Jones, and Joan C. Tronto, 1–12. New York: New York University Press.

Collins, Patricia Hill. 1990. *Black Feminist Thought: Knowledge, Consciousness, and the Politics of Empowerment*. Boston: Unwin Hyman.

Dill, Bonnie Thornton. 1994. "Fictive Kin, Paper Sons, and Compadrazgo: Women of Color and the Struggle for Family Survival." In *Women of Color in U.S. Society*, ed. Maxine Baca Zinn and Bonnie Thornton Dill, 149–69. Philadelphia: Temple University Press.

Espiritu, Yen L. 1997. "Race, Gender, Class in the Lives of Asian American." *Race, Gender, and Class* 4, no. 3: 12–19.

Friedman, Debra, and Doug McAdam. 1992. "Collective Identity and Activism: Networks, Choices, and the Life of a Social Movement." In *Frontiers in Social Movement Theory*, ed. Aldon D. Morris and Carol McClurg Mueller, 156–73. New Haven: Yale University Press.

Glenn, Evelyn Nakano. 1992. "From Servitude to Service Work: Historical Continuities in the Racial Division of Paid Reproductive Labor." *Signs: Journal of Women in Culture and Society* 18: 1–43.

Gonzalez, Juan. 2000. *Harvest of Empire: A History of Latinos in America.* New York: Viking.

Goode, Judith and Jo Anne Schneider. 1994. *Reshaping Ethnic and Racial Relations in Philadelphia: Immigrants in A Divided City*. Philadelphia: Temple University Press.

Gouglas, Michael. 1996. "Multilingual Education on the Table." *San Gabriel Valley Tribune*, June 11, A3.

Hardy-Fanta, Carol. 1993. *Latina Politics, Latino Politics: Gender, Culture, and Political Participation*. Philadelphia: Temple University Press.

Krauss, Celene. 1998. "Women of Color on the Front Lines." In *Race, Class, and Gender: An Anthology*, ed. Margaret L. Anderson and Patricia Hill Collins. Belmont, CA: Wadsworth.

Lamphere, Louise. 1992. "Introduction: The Shaping of Diversity." In *Structuring Diversity: Ethnographic Perspectives in the New Immigration*, ed. Louise Lamphere, 1–34. Chicago: University of Chicago Press.

Martínez, Elizabeth. 1998. *De Colores Means All of Us: Latina Views for a Multi-Colored Century*. Boston: South End.

Méndez-Negrete, Josephine. 1999. "Awareness, Consciousness, and Resistance: Raced, Classed, and Gendered Leadership Implications in Milagro, California." *Frontiers: A Journal of Women Studies* 20, no. 1: 24–44.

Naples, Nancy A. 1998. *Grassroots Warriors: Activist Mothering, Community Work, and the War on Poverty.* New York: Routledge, 1998.

Ochoa, Gilda Laura. 1999. "Everyday Ways of Resistance and Cooperation: Mexican American Women Building *Puentes* with Immigrants." *Frontiers: A Journal of Women Studies* 20, no. 1: 1–20.

———. Forthcoming. *Becoming Neighbors: Power, Conflict, and Solidarity in a Mexican American Community.* Austin, TX: University of Texas Press.

Pardo, Mary. 1998. *Mexican American Women Activists: Identity and Resistance in Two Los Angeles Communities.* Philadelphia: Temple University Press.

———. 1991. "Creating Community: Mexican American Women in Eastside Los Angeles." *Aztlan* 20 no. 1–2: 39–71.

Shannon, Sheila M. 1996. "Minority Parental Involvement: A Mexican Mother's Experience and a Teacher's Interpretation." *Education and Urban Society* 29, no. 1: 71–84.

Shannon, Sheila M., and Silvia Lojero Latimer. 1996. "Latino Parent Involvement in Schools: A Story of Struggle and Resistance." *Journal of Educational Issues of Language Minority Students* 13: 301–19.

Soldatenko, María. 1991. "Organizing Latina Garment Workers in Los Angeles." *Aztlan* 20, no. 1–2: 87–95.

Zavella, Patricia. 1987. *Women's Work and Chicano Families: Cannery Workers of the Santa Clara Valley.* Ithaca, NY: Cornell University Press.

PART IV

SOCIAL ISSUES IN THE CHICANO/MEXICANO COMMUNITY

8

Of *Corridos* and Convicts: *Gringo* (In)Justice in Early Border Ballads and Contemporary *Pinto* Poetry

Raúl Homero Villa

a great many men and women who up till then would never have thought of producing a literary work, now that they find themselves in exceptional circumstances—in prison, with the Maquis, or on the eve of their execution—feel the need to speak to their nation, to compose the sentence which expresses the heart of the people, and to become the mouthpiece of a new reality in action.[1]

—Frantz Fanon, *The Wretched of the Earth*

TWO HOLLYWOOD FILMS THAT FEATURE CHICANOS in and around the prison system have brought to mass cultural view an experience long known to the Chicano population but not recognized, much less understood, by the general U.S. public. Edward James Olmos's *American Me* (1991) and Taylor Hackford's *Bound By Honor* (1993) have, in different ways, cast light on the complex subculture of the *pinto*, or Chicano prisoner. Neither film is squeamish in its representation of the violence inherent to this subculture. *American Me* is particularly relentless in this respect, as part of Olmos's stated intention to scare young Chicanos away from *la vida loca* (the crazy life). But violence is not the only aspect of the *pinto* experience represented in the films. In both productions, there are important *pinto* characters whose sense of their condition as prisoners includes a sociopolitical consciousness. This consciousness acknowledges that Chicanos, along with African Americans, constitute a disproportionately large percentage of the U.S. prison population. Such knowledge, however, does not point to an innate Chicano propensity for crime, but rather identifies the effects of the Chicano community's generally subordinate social and economic status in a structure of racially organized power in this country.

The point to be made, therefore, is that justice is *not* blind, despite the official rhetoric of the U.S. judicial and penal systems. The experience of *gringo* (in)justice has been a constant fact of Chicano history as well as a continuing theme of Chicano expressive culture. In this chapter, I plot a continuum between popular balladry in early Chicano culture and the contestative expressions of recent Chicano and Chicana prison poetry. I argue that the earlier ballads functioned retrospectively as a cultural taproot for the contemporary writers, providing models of social criticism, thematic strategies, and narrative or generic conventions that are adapted and transformed by socially critical *pinto* poets.

Intercultural Conflict: The Historical Context of Border Balladry and Critical *Pinto* Poetry

As Américo Paredes has ably demonstrated, the historical relations of *mexicano* and Anglo-American communities in what is the now the U.S. Southwest have led *mexicanos* to produce a wealth of folklore whose dominant theme is "intercultural conflict."[2] In expressions as diverse as cross-cultural/out-group naming (and name-calling), jokes, and popular songs, *mexicanos* fashioned popular cultural forms that creatively mediated their experiences and opinions of contact and conflict with the growing population and culture of *los gringos*.

The premier expressive practice to take up the theme of intercultural conflict was undoubtedly the *corrido*, or ballad tradition. The reasons for its primacy as a popular symbolic practice have been well documented.[3] *Corridos* were used to tell stories about any events of consequence or curiosity for the *mexicano* community, ranging from natural disasters to train robberies to military battles. However, during the period of *corrido* ascendancy (approximately 1836–1930) its narrative repertoire focused increasingly toward "one theme, the border conflict; [and] one concept of the hero, the man[4] fighting for his right with his pistol in his hand."[5] Self-defense, however, is only part of the reason compelling the hero of the border conflict. He is almost always motivated to fight for the rights of fellow Mexicans as well as his own rights. Examples include Gregorio Cortez, who killed two Texas sheriffs after one of them shot his brother; Jacinto Treviño, who avenges his brother's death by killing several Americans; Rito García, who shoots several Anglo officers for unlawfully searching his home and harassing its residents; and Aniceto Pizaña, whose band of *sediciosos* (seditionists) set out to overthrow Anglo-

American rule in South Texas.[6] The *corrido* and its border Mexican audience identified the individual hero's plight as representative of the repression increasingly experienced (in proportion to the increase of the Anglo-American population in the U.S. Southwest) by the collective Mexican-descent population. In this way the *corrido*, in its epic heroic genre, provided the first sustained popular narrativization of the Chicano experience of *gringo* (in)justice within the imposed borders of the U.S. Southwest.

In its glorification of the hero's armed response to the *rinche* (Texas Rangers) violation of his own or his community's civil and human rights, the *corrido* narrativized popular Mexican wisdom regarding the Anglo-American legal establishment. In "Rito García," for example, the hero wisely reasons,

Conociendo bien las leyes	(Knowing well how the law works
del país americano,	in the American nation,
me pasé a buscar abrigo	I went in search of refuge
a mi suelo mexicano.	on my own Mexican soil.)

And when he is later tried in a Texas court:

Allí no alcancé clemencia,	(There I found no mercy,
ni me quisieron oír,	they didn't even listen to me,
pues voy a la penitencía	now I'll go to prison
enternamente a sufrir.	and suffer all my life.
. . . . . .	. . . . . .
. . . voy a la penitencía	. . . I'm going to prison
por defender mi derecho.[7]	for defending my rights.)

The heroic narrative tradition has produced the most potent and lasting *corridos* of social conflict and resistance. At a more fundamental level, the existence of the present United States–Mexico border, already a major condition of possibility for the heroic *corrido* genre, became a fundamental theme and narrative element in the creative mediations of intercultural conflict.

In a purely practical sense, the formation of a new geopolitical boundary line between the United States and Mexico in 1848 required, from the Anglo-American perspective, that it be regulated, administered, and policed. The border line itself, marking the defeat of Mexico in the Mexican–American War, became for *mexicanos* on both sides another violation under the rubric of intercultural conflict. Consider, as Américo Paredes describes it, that when the Rio Grande "became a dividing line instead of a focus for normal activity, it broke apart an area that had once been a unified homeland. People ended up with friends and relatives living in what had legally become a foreign land, hedged in by all kinds of immigration and customs restrictions."[8] The disruption of kinship and community networks, of the normal forms of social intercourse and commerce, was understood by many border Mexicans as a related violation to the violent physical assaults by the *rinches*. As such, "illegal activities" that undermined U.S. regulation of border transit and exchange were often represented in *mexicano* folklore as forms of incipient rebellion whereby the "smuggler, the illegal alien looking for work, and the border-conflict hero became identified in the popular mind. They came in conflict with the same American laws and often with the same individual officers of the law, who were all looked upon as *rinches*."[9] Such perceptions expressed a clear logic of resistance. The folkloric idealization of the smuggler and "illegal alien" rhetorically subverted official government definitions of criminality. Furthermore, equating officers of the law with *rinches* semantically identified U.S. enforcement agencies with the oppressiveness of the *rinches*.

In the *corrido* poetics of intercultural conflict, there is an intuitive articulation of dissent from Anglo-American discourses and categories of justice and legality. These social poetics also contain thematic elements and discursive strategies that would be taken up by critically conscious *pinto* poets. In the dominant heroic narrative, for example, although the fate of the hero was often violent death at the hands of a large posse of *rinches*, imprisonment was sometimes the result, as in the case of Rito García, cited above, and Gregorio Cortez, the most famous *corrido* hero.

Although Cortez was drawn into violent retribution and flight because of the unjust shooting of his brother by a Texas sheriff, he was not shot in the field of action but tried in a court of law. "Rito García," which precedes "Gregorio Cortez" by sixteen years, alludes to the actual trial experience. García, quite aware of the *rinches*' "field justice," and "knowing well how the law works in the United States" fled to Mexico. But when he was betrayed and sent back to American authorities, his intuition about the U.S. legal system was borne out: "I found no clemency there; they would not even listen to me."[10]

The hero's sense of inevitable guilt in the U.S. legal system resurfaces constantly in later *pinto* poetry as a politicized popular insight, fueled by the escalated Chicano-police conflict of the urban barrios. Raúl Salinas expresses this sensibility powerfully in his classic poem "Un Trip Through the Mind Jail":

> Ratón: 20 years for a matchbox of weed. Is that cold?
> No lawyer   no jury   no trial   i'm guilty
> Aren't we all guilty?[11]

The interrogative "Is that cold?" asks a rhetorical question: "Is this what you call justice?" Of course, disproportionate punishment, with scarce recourse to fair judicial process, is what passes for justice in the experience of many Chicanos.[12] The commonness of this experience in the modern barrio allows Ratón's "cold" experience to represent another instance of the individual-collective nexus that made the *corrido* such a potent symbolic expression of its audience's cultural, group perspective: If "i'm guilty/Aren't we all guilty?"

The poetic expressions of an individual-collective nexus often mirrored the actual involvement of the Chicano community in key legal conflicts that were then creatively rendered in oral and literary texts. In the case of the greatest *corrido* hero, Gregorio Cortez, the lyrical narrative ends precisely where the historical narrative of his community's activism begins: when he is brought to trial. His legal battles over the next three years were no less dramatic than his pursuit and capture. Although only one man was on trial, the larger Chicano community became a collective protagonist, with their efforts leading to not only support for Cortez's defense but the formation of a number of tentative civic organizations that lasted beyond the trial and appeal process. According to Américo Paredes, "Gregorio Cortez and the *corrido* about him are a milestone in the Mexican-American's emerging group consciousness. . . . The readiness with which Mexicans in the United States came together in his defense showed that the necessary conditions existed for united effort."[13]

In 1942, the mass trial of Chicano "gang" youths for the murder of José Díaz, popularly known as the "case of Sleepy Lagoon," revealed similar conditions for united effort. The Sleepy Lagoon Defense Committee, a broad-based coalition of Chicanos and sympathetic non-Chicanos, carried on its battle in the face of legal proceedings that have been amply documented as a farce of justice and due process.[14] This case deserves particular mention here not simply because of the sensational nature of the events or its notable place in the Chicano historical and popular imagination. Of equal or greater significance is the very way in which the charges were made. Not one, or even a few, but twenty-two members of the 38th Street Club were accused of criminal conspiracy. By the logic of this collective accusation, every defendant, even if he had nothing to do with the Díaz killing, could be charged with his death. Guilt by cultural association was never so clearly and officially revealed.[15] Alfredo Mirandé, in his book *Gringo Justice*, appropriately titled a chapter on this case, "Sleepy Lagoon: The Chicano Community on Trial."[16] In the trial of Gregorio Cortez, the Chicano community understood and reacted to the collective resonances of an individual Chicano's battle with the Anglo-American legal system. Conversely, the Sleepy Lagoon case exposed the ideological notion that Mexicans were culturally prone to criminal violence. This view, which traced Chicanos' supposed blood lust back to the sacrificial practices of Aztec society, was openly expressed in a report presented by Captain E. Duran Myers, chief of the Los Angeles County Sheriff's Office Foreign Relations Bureau, to the grand jury investigating "Mexican juvenile delinquency" at the time of the trial.[17] The

Chicano community *was* on trial, as the mass indictments and inflammatory Mexican-baiting yellow journalism made painfully evident to Chicanos in Los Angeles and elsewhere. The oppressive truism critiqued by Raúl Salinas (i'm guilty/Aren't we all guilty?") was presaged by such historical evidence as this.

From *La Penitencia* to *La Pinta:* Traditional Visions and Critical Revisions of the Prison Experience

Thus far we have considered certain themes and socially critical insights, produced within and against the history of intercultural border conflict, given their first sustained narrativization in the heroic tradition of the *corrido*, and carried on in recent Chicano prisoner poetry. This comparative analysis suggests a partial history of the folkloric roots of contemporary Chicano literature. However, in order to specify the particular genealogy of *pinto* poetics, we must identify *corrido* accounts of the prison experience itself as they contribute to the larger master narrative of intercultural conflict. Though the examples are far fewer than the dominant heroic narratives, the prisoner *corrido* is a specific precursor to critical *pinto* poetry. In rare instances as well, the heroic *corrido* may allude to the prison experience. "Rito García," for example, includes two brief references to the hero's impending penitentiary fate (though it does not substantially reflect on his actual imprisonment). To its credit, the text reveals one anticipated detail of imprisonment, which at first reading or listening might seem to be a generic figure of speech:

Me voy a la penitencia,	(I'm going to prison,
Porque así lo quiso la suerte,	as luck would have it,
voy a arrastrar la cadena	I'll be dragging a chain
hasta que venga la muerte.[18]	until the day I die.)

Considering the *rinche* field justice usually meted out to the border conflict hero, García's prison sentence substitutes a death-in-stasis for a death-in-flight. This notion of imprisonment as a form of death-in-life figures prominently in much of the critical *pinto* tradition. Lorrie Martínez provides a compelling example of this institutional violation of the *pinto*.

> There's nothing left to say.
> I will die a slow death,
>
> they have tortured my mind
> physically my body is
> bruised and my heart is cold.
>
> In the smoke I could
> Smell the dead bodies . . .[19]

Raúl Salinas composed a eulogy for a fellow *pinto*:

> . . . he died . . .
> years later—
> in the putrefying bowels
> of a dismal prison—
> death's impact
> SLAPS!
> the face of consciousness
> and jars the torpid brain
> AWAKE![20]

Américo Paredes has described how the "prisoner's song usually shows us the protagonist in his cell, yearning for his sweetheart or mother, counting the prison bars or listening for the footsteps of the executioner—all the while consoled by an angel or little bird."[21] He also notes the prisoner's characteristic repentance or regret for his criminal activity. These elements compose a narrative genre of the prisoner's sorrows. This genre is typically void of the explicit social critique present in the border-hero narratives, tending mostly toward a confessional melodrama. Significant exceptions exist, however, in which a prisoner *corrido* manifests a clear critique of the U.S. judicial system. "Manuel Garza de León" is such an exception, since as Paredes argues, it

> is not much about the "sorrows of the prisoner" as it is about the intercultural conditions that have put the protagonist behind the bars. A man goes to prison under laws he had no part in making, according to concepts of justice he does not understand. He feels that he is in prison . . . because he is a Mexican . . . It was not a judge who sentenced Manuel to thirty years; it was an "American." And the prison guards who harass him with their dogs are called *rinches* too.[22]

The *corrido* of "Manuel Garza de León," which dates from around 1915, is a precursory model for reading socially critical *pinto* writing. Unlike the typical prisoner ballad, this one expresses a critical insight, in the best tradition of the heroic *corrido*, that lays bare the overdetermined racial ideologies in the dominant discourses and practices of justice and punishment. In light of this popular critique, which would be quite apparent to the ballad's native audience, even the melodramatic details that describes the suffering of the prisoner and his loved ones serve a critical cause by highlighting the subjective, emotional effects of this injustice.

While there are countless examples of the uncritical use of sentimentality by contemporary *pinto* poets, many follow the example of "Manuel Garza de León" by using the melodramatic *corrido* conventions in the service of a social critique. Sometimes this takes the form of directly evoking a precursory *corrido* text. In "EXISTIR ES . . . an experiment in writing in and around a few

songs from the *barrio*" Ricardo Sánchez uses, among other songs, "El Contra-
bando de El Paso" as a counterpoint in narrating his quest for a Chicano identity.[23] Sánchez freely associates with images from this *corrido* of a prisoner's
laments, using them as impressionistic punctuation to his own existential
odyssey. For example, when "oblivion loomed on the horizon as my only destination," he evokes the *corrido* protagonist's own question of destination, "le
pregunto a mister hill / que si vamos pa' luisiana," while the train in the *corrido* recalls how "the train of my thoughts still rannnnnn on and on."[24] Similarly, the *corrido* protagonist's sentencing to Leavenworth evokes how Sánchez
"was enclosed in a prison of inculcated hates" and in an actual prison.

More common than the suturing of a traditional *corrido* text into the *pinto*
text is the reworking of the prisoner ballad's generic elements in the narrative
and thematic poetics of the *pinto* text. Two related, generic elements have been
consistently transformed in this way. One is the force and meaning of grief, in
both the prisoner's lament and (generally) the mother's sorrow; the other is
the tone of moralism or moral censure. In the traditional melodramatic narrative, the prisoner's lament is often focused on a twin regret: first, of the
painful fate that has befallen him and, second, of the pain he has caused his
loved ones, especially his mother. The latter motif is evident in "El Contra-
bando de El Paso," when the convict narrator typically seeks his "madre
idolatrada / [para] pedirle la bendición" ("beloved mother / [to] ask for her
blessing"), or concludes with an offering of his affection (and of his song, as
well), as if in reparation for his filial shortcomings: "Ahi te dejo, mamacita, /
un suspiro y un abrazo" (Mother of mine, / I leave you a sigh and an em-
brace").[25] Raúl Salinas, in the dedication that opens his book, *Un Trip through
the Mind Jail Y Otras Excursiones,*[26] invokes a similar appeal in offering the
poems to his mother:

> Amá, whether you read
> this or not;
> Here's hoping
> it makes up
> for
> the graduation picture
> (cap / gown & diploma)
> that never graced
> your class-confusing
> cuarto de sala.

Even as he employs a conventional motif, he transforms it by using it to illustrate a political critique of U.S. foreign policy. For example, later in the dedication, he asks his mother to accept his poem as compensation:

> Also, for the
> lack of first-after-
> basic training
> photos proving
> involvement in
> immoral wars.[27]

Luis Talamántez, in "Reflections of a Convict,"[28] engages a sustained meditation on the cultural-critical wisdom born of the suffering of his "aged abuela." The principal lesson of her wisdom, not surprisingly, is the knowledge of intercultural conflict. From her own experience she came to know:

> The ways of the pale foreigners
> In our land and our way of life
> 　　　always the bringer of our troubles
> . . . the inquisitors
> Beckoning to us with their crook'd finger
> their rednecks and *panzas* swollen with poisons
> . . . of greed and consumption—their eyes hard like hearts . . .
> calling us to come to them
> To be abused, used and screwed.[29]

This socially critical knowledge is further illustrated by the intimate violation of her own family's wholeness by the military and judicial institution of the U.S. government.

> It was not enough that they had taken
> Grandma's sons away to war—
> But that they they've taken her grandsons
> To jail . . .
> 　　　. . . . . .
> No one would think to convince grandma that the *gringo*
> did not take her son away . . . long ago
> Just to leave him far away . . . on Iwo Jima
> 　　　. . . . . .
> No one can tell her that the *gringo*
> does not have her *nieto* prisoner
> hurting him silently as our people
> have learned to be hurt and defeated
> keeping him
> so that she may never see him again either.[30]

Here Talamántez shows that the *abuela*'s grief is not simply an emotional response to overwhelming circumstances, a powerless response to a fate beyond her control. Her lament reveals an experiential political consciousness in which a pointed ideological critique of "gringo" institutional practices is expressed in an emotive register.

This critical articulation of grief is a revision of the generic lament that is its precursor, for in the traditional narration of the mother's (and the prisoner's) grief, *fortuna* (fate), *destino* (destiny), *suerte* (luck), and *la mano de Dios* (the hand, or will, of God) figure prominently as explanations for being imprisoned. We may recall here Rito Garciá's statement that "asi lo quiso la suerte." Implicit in the traditional narrative, then, is a resignation or sense of acceptance that precludes any questioning of the possible racial and political overdeterminations of the prisoner's "fate." Quite the contrary, in Talamántez's poem, the *abuela* knows only too clearly that her grief does not respond to heavenly whims but to concrete institutional practices (prison, the draft) acting against her family and her community.

The revision of popular, or "typical," perceptions as critical consciousness is central to the strategic intention of socially conscious *pinto* writing. Raúl Salinas, for one, shows the traditional unreflective resignation of the mother in "Un Trip."

> Indian mothers, too unaware
> of courtroom tragic-comedies
> folded arms across their bosoms
> saying, "*sea por Dios*" [It's God's will].[31]

only to subvert such religious mystifications elsewhere:

> And so, dear friend & brother
> The System
> (not God!)
>   created you . . .
> that system
>   took
>   you
>   away.[32]

As Salinas sets up a tension between an uncritical popular perception (the will of God) and his own critical perception of "The System," so too do other *pintos* inscribe this tension in the relations between characters in their poems, textualizing the consciousness-raising that their poems hope to spark in the reader.

In "A Visit with Mama"[33] Pancho Aguila confronts, consoles, and tries to convert the "misery / my mother cries about," by redirecting her grief through a critical social analysis:

> . . . I tell her
> the misery is in the world—
> I am not the beast—
> the beast lives on the outside
> devouring the country

By inverting the moral and critical hierarchies embedded in his mother's misery, the poet offers a transformative vision of a reconstructed social landscape:

> I tell her, cheer up
> the sweet wine
> clears against the sun.
> All my visions
> are a marble of song
> sculpting the temple
> in offering to a new world.

Similarly, in "Mt. Tamalpais,"[34] the protagonist must reconcile the memory of his *tío*'s view of prison with his own socially critical perspective born of "nearly nine years of prison / in the waters of life."

> Over-looking San Quentin
> where my Tío Tonio once told me,
> "Bad men live there."
> Now, listening to the comrade teacher,
> "Many revolutionaries come from prison."

Such inversions of a dominant moral hierarchy voiced in the common sense of Tío Tonio ("Bad men live there.") is a major critical thrust of the contestative *pinto* tradition. This tradition employs a radical, oppositional method of reinterpreting many pronouncements of dominant American social discourse to uncover their ideological biases. In their poetics, these *pintos* are, as José D. Saldívar has noted of other Chicano poetry, "offering concrete theories of social resistance."[35] This oppositional poetics is powerfully employed by Raúl Salinas in "El Tecato."[36] Salinas evokes the dominant moral rhetoric that is applied to the *tecato* (junkie) and then with biting irony juxtaposes it to his unflagging paternal responsibility:

> that scourge . . . that social leper
> beamed with pride
> because he knew he could
> (in spite of sickness)
> well provide [for his children].[37]

Salinas then gives a more accurate and humane assessment of the *tecato* as

> a sick, addicted father/brother/son,
> who recognized his children's need
> for food and nourishment
> while no one recognized his need
> for drugs and treatment[38]

And yet, to subvert the moralistic judgments applied to the *tecato* is not enough, for the actual life history of Elías Perales, on which the poem is based, shows us how the social power of moralistic rhetoric can transcend semantics in the exercise of deadly material force:

> So the predators [narcotics officers] gunned him down
> in the manner of that social madness
> that runs rampant across the land,
> dressing itself in the finery & raiments of
> JUSTIFIABLE HOMICIDE!!![39]

These indeed are the empire's new clothes, its discursive "finery & raiments," nakedly revealed by Salinas's penetrating critical vision.

Clearly, Salinas dismantles the duplicitous facade of dominant legal and moral rhetorics, exposing to view some tragic effects of their institutional enforcements.

Such discrepancies between U.S. dominant discourses and the real-life experiences of oppressed people exemplifies the sort of compelling duplicities that similarly inspired *corridistas* to make cultural heroes of so-called criminals and bandits. In the poetics of these *corridistas* and *pintos*, laying bare what the dominant discourse really says is the first step toward what Fanon described as "a new reality in action."[40]

Notes

1. Frantz Fanon, *The Wretched of the Earth* (New York: Grove, 1963), 223.

2. Américo Paredes, *A Texas-Mexican Cancionero: Folksongs of the Lower Border* (Urbana: University of Illinois Press, 1976); Paredes, *"With His Pistol in His Hand": A Border Ballad and Its Hero* (1958; Austin: University of Texas Press, 1982).

3. José E. Limón, "The Rise, Fall and 'Revival' of the Mexican-American Ballad: A Review Essay," *Studies in Latin American Popular Culture*, 2 (1983): 202–7; Paredes, *"With His Pistol in His Hand"*; John Holmes McDowell, "The *Corrido* of Greater Mexico Discourse, Music and Event," in Richard Bauman and Roger D. Abrahams, eds., *"And Other Neighborly Names": Social Processes and Cultural Image Folklore* (Austin: University of Texas Press, 1981), 44–75.

4. The hero of border conflict was invariably male, showing a clear patriarchal, or male-dominant, perspective in the genre. This perspective assumed that it was predominately, if not exclusively, a man's role to act publicly, and often violently, to defend himself as well as "his" family, "his" property, and "his" land. Befitting such a gendered bias, women in *corridos* were typically invisible, made dependent on a man, or, in the worst cases, figured as treacherous. For an analysis of the representation of women in the *corrido* tradition, see María Herrera-Sobek, *The Mexican Corrido: A Feminist Analysis* (Bloomington: Indiana University Press, 1990).

5. Paredes, "*With His Pistol in His Hand,*" 149.

6. Pizaña unsuccessfully attempted to establish a Spanish-speaking republic in South Texas in 1915 using guerrilla insurgency and appeals to other racial minority groups throughout the Southwest as his principal actions. His appeal to coalition and armed rebellion was laid out in a document called "El plan de San Diego," named after the town of San Diego, Texas, from which he launched his campaign.

7. Transcribed in Paredes, *Texas-Mexican Cancionero*, 58. The translations in this chapter are my own.

8. Paredes, *Texas-Mexican Cancionero*, 43.

9. Américo Paredes, "The Problem of Identity in a Changing Culture: Popular Expressions of Culture Conflict along the Lower Rio Grande Border," in Stanley R. Ross, ed., *Views across the Border: The United States and Mexico* (Albuquerque: University of New Mexico Press, 1978), 75.

10. Transcribed in Paredes, *Texas-Mexican Cancionero*, 59.

11. Raúl R. Salinas, *Un Trip through the Mind Jail Y Otras Excursiones* (San Francisco: Editorial Pocho-Che, 1980), 58–59.

12. Armando Morales, *Ando Sangrando (I Am Bleeding): A Study of Mexican American-Police Conflict* (La Puente, CA: Perspective, 1972).

13. Paredes, *Texas-Mexican Cancionero*, 31.

14. Carey McWilliams, *North from Mexico: The Spanish-Speaking People of the United States* (New York: Greenwood, 1948), 228–33; Alfredo Mirandé, *Gringo Justice* (Notre Dame, IN: Notre Dame University Press, 1987), 156–72; Rodolfo Acuña, *Occupied America: A History of Chicanos*, 3rd ed. (New York: Harper & Row, 1988), 255–56.

15. The charges of criminal conspiracy were never upheld, although seventeen of the defendants were found guilty of a variety of crimes ranging from assault to first-degree murder. The battle for justice by the Sleepy Lagoon Defense Committee, however, brought about a unanimous decision on appeal reversing all the lower court rulings, but only after the defendants had spent nearly two years in jail, unable to procure the necessary bail during the long appeal process. In Rodolfo Acuña, *Occupied America*, 255–56.

16. Alfredo Mirandé, *Gringo Justice.*

17. McWilliams, *North from Mexico*, 233–35.

18. Transcribed in Paredes, *Texas-Mexican Cancionero*, 58. My emphasis.

19. Lorri Martínez, "Slow Death," *Where Eagles Fall* (Brunswick, ME: Blackberry, 1982), n.p.

20. Raúl R. Salinas, "In Memoriam: Riche," *Un Trip through the Mind Jail,* 49–50.

21. Paredes, *Texas-Mexican Cancionero*, 44.

22. Paredes, *Texas-Mexican Cancionero,* 44–45.

23. Ricardo Sánchez, *Canto y grito mi liberación* (Garden City, NY: Anchor, 1973), 144–53.

24. Sánchez, *Canto y grito mi liberación,* 152.

25. Paredes, *Texas-Mexican Cancionero,* 104.

26. Salinas, *Un Trip through the Mind Jail.*

27. Salinas, "Dedicatoria," *Un Trip through the Mind Jail,* 16.

28. Luis Talamántez, "Reflections of a Convict," *Bilingual Review* 4, no. 1–2 (1977): 123–25. Reprinted with permission of copyright holder, Bilingual Press/Editorial Bilingüe, Arizona State University, Tempe, AZ.

29. Talamántez, "Reflections of a Convict," 123.

30. Talamántez, "Reflections of a Convict," 124–25.

31. Salinas, *Un Trip through the Mind Jail,* 60.

32. Salinas, *Un Trip through the Mind Jail,* 49–50.

33. Pancho Aguila, *11 Poems.* Chapbook published as part of *Mango,* 1, no. 3–4: n.p.

34. Aguila, *11 Poems,* n.p.

35. José David Saldívar, "Towards a Chicano Poetics: The Making of the Chicano subject, 1969-1982," *Confluencia: Revista Hispánica de Cultura y Literatura* 1, no. 2 (1986): 10–17; 10.

36. Salinas, *Un Trip through the Mind Jail,* 52.

37. Salinas, *Un Trip through the Mind Jail,* 52.

38. Salinas, *Un Trip through the Mind Jail,* 52.

39. Salinas, *Un Trip through the Mind Jail,* 52.

40. Fanon, *Wretched of the Earth,* 223.

References

Acuña, Rodolfo. 1988. *Occupied America: A History of Chicanos.* 3d ed. New York: Harper & Row.

Aguila, Pancho. N.d. *11 Poems.* Chapbook published as part of *Mango,* 1, no. 3–4: n.p.

Fanon, Frantz. 1963. *The Wretched of the Earth.* New York: Grove.

Herrera-Sobek, María. 1990. *The Mexican Corrido: A Feminist Analysis.* Bloomington: Indiana University Press.

Limón, José E. 1983. "The Rise, Fall, and 'Revival' of the Mexican-American Ballad: A Review Essay." *Studies in Latin American Popular Culture* 2: 202–7.

Martínez, Lorri. 1982. "Slow Death." In *Where Eagles Fall.* Brunswick, ME: Blackberry.

McDowell, John Holmes. 1981. "The *Corrido* of Greater Mexico Discourse, Music and Event." In *"And Other Neighborly Names": Social Processes and Cultural Image Folklore,* ed. Richard Bauman and Roger D. Abrahams, 44–75. Austin, TX: University of Texas Press.

McWilliams, Carey. 1948. *North from Mexico: The Spanish-Speaking People of the United States.* New York: Greenwood.

Mirandé, Alfredo. 1987. *Gringo Justice.* Notre Dame, IN: Notre Dame University Press.

Morales, Armando. 1972. *Ando Sangrando (I Am Bleeding): A Study of Mexican American-Police Conflict.* La Puente, CA: Perspective.

Paredes, Américo. 1976. *A Texas-Mexican Cancionero: Folksongs of the Lower Border.* Urbana: University of Illinois Press.

———. 1978. "The Problem of Identity in a Changing Culture: Popular Expressions of Culture Conflict along the Lower Rio Grande Border." In *Views across the Border: The United States and Mexico,* ed. Stanley R. Ross, 75. Albuquerque: University of New Mexico Press.

———. 1982. *"With His Pistol in His Hand": A Border Ballad and Its Hero.* Austin, TX: University of Texas Press. Originally published in 1958.

Saldívar, José David. 1986. "Towards a Chicano Poetics: The Making of the Chicano Subject, 1969–1982." *Confluencia: Revista hispánica de cultura y literatura* 1–2, no. 10: 10–17.

Salinas, Raúl R. 1980. *Un Trip through the Mind Jail Y Otras Excursiones,* 58–59. San Francisco, CA: Editorial Pocho-Che.

Sánchez, Ricardo. 1973. *Canto y grito mi liberación.* Garden City, NY: Anchor.

Talamántez, Luis. 1977. "Reflections of a Convict." *Bilingual Review* 4, no. 1–2: 123–25. Reprinted with permission of copyright holder, Bilingual Press/Editorial Bilingüe, Arizona State University, Tempe, AZ.

9

Festejando Community: Celebrating Fiesta Mexicana in Woodburn, Oregon

Elizabeth Flores

F ESTIVALS HAVE BECOME A MODERN-DAY PERFORMANCE GENRE in many ethnic communities, big and small. For many ethnic groups, these events grow out of grassroots organizational efforts to preserve heritage, celebrate the native country's calendar events, and share with host communities to build bridges and promote a better understanding. Festivals are events that "occur at calendrically regulated intervals and are public in nature, participatory in ethos, complex in structure, and multiple in voice, scene, and purpose" (Stoeltje 1992, 261). Often these festivals foster a forum for the construction and communication of identities at the local, regional, and national levels.

Celebrating our heritage and culture feeds our cultural souls, gives fervor to a part of us that resonates in our everyday life and existence. When we celebrate our cultural events, we pay tribute to our roots, we affirm our heritage, and we share traditions with those who are willing to partake in our rituals, traditions, food, music, and cultural artifacts.

This chapter examines the relevance of celebrating Fiesta Mexicana in Woodburn, Oregon. Fiesta demonstrates the importance of celebrating one's culture by way of affirming the presence of the Mexican American/Mexican community in Woodburn in order to solidify its history as part of Woodburn's collective past. The fiesta's significance and relevance goes beyond cultural foods, traditional dances, and mariachi music. The fiesta is a central place to observe a culture evolve, a forum for relationships to be fostered, and a place to watch the multidynamics of the Latino culture. This chapter chronicles the beginnings of the fiesta in the past forty years and the transformation that it has gone through in the wake of the changing demographic trends for Oregon.

Moreover, the fiesta is an indication of how Latinos in this region have gone from a Texan Mexican to a Mexican American migrant population to a strong Mexican immigrant population. The cultural nuances of the fiesta reflect a change in the Latino population of Woodburn. Yet, given the subtle differences among these different but similar ethnic subgroups, cultural cohesiveness prevails and the fiesta is a nucleus of community cohesiveness for all Latinos who reside in Woodburn.

Woodburn, Oregon, is located approximately thirty miles south of Portland in Marion County, which is located in the Willamette Valley, where 70 percent of Oregon's population resides. The valley is highly conducive to field crops, greenhouse and nursery crops, orchard crops, and livestock. Factors that make Oregon diverse and rich in farm commodities are "rainfall, temperature, growing season, soils, proximity to population centers, and access to economic infrastructures" (Loy et al. 2001, 96). This community has grown significantly in the past forty to fifty years. It is one of the areas of western Oregon to see Mexican American pioneers from Texas starting in the 1950s. Miguel Salinas, a longtime resident of the Willamette Valley, applies the term "pioneer" to the families that came during this era. Salinas has been an organizer, activist, educator, and has contributed to various communities throughout the years. The interviews that he has granted greatly contribute to this chapter in recording and analyzing the oral history of the fiesta. Salinas explains that "during the 1950s there were no Spanish surname families in the valley. Due to these families being the first Latino families to settle in these parts this has earned them the term 'pioneers.'" These Latino families were not "pioneers" in the Anglo covered wagon tradition but first-time Latino settlers in the valley. There already were people of color in the valley, such as Filipinos, Chinese, and African Americans, but not Latinos. Marion County became the cradle of the Latino/Tejano presence. As a result of the Tejano presence in Woodburn, generations have stayed on and formed part of the traditions like fiesta. This celebration strengthens ethnic and nationalist pride in a geographic area that is isolated from many of these people's origins like the Southwest, California, and even Mexico.

Genesis of Woodburn

An Anglo-American, Jesse H. Settlemier, founded Woodburn. He came as a young boy with his father, George Settlemier, who was an ardent farmworker dedicated to cultivation and greenhouse plants. At the age of nineteen, Jesse bought eighty acres of land and started to develop the first four blocks of a new city on the land and thus founded the city of Woodburn. In 1870, Oregon and California built a railroad to connect San Francisco and Portland. The four blocks of this new city ran alongside the railway. Because the goal was to see the city grow, Settlemier offered sections of the city to anyone who would build a house on the land.

As the city of Woodburn began to take shape in 1885, the first school was established. In 1888 journalists began writing for the *Woodburn Independent*. In 1889 the city was incorporated and by 1893, it had 1,200 inhabitants; by 1925, that number rose to 2,000. In 1989 Woodburn celebrated its centennial with 12,000 inhabitants. The population grew again when Interstate 5 was built to pass through the west side of town (*El Hispanic News y Más* 2002).

The city of Woodburn has enjoyed diversity since about 1,000 Orthodox Russians arrived in the area in the 1960s. During the 1950s Latinos, mostly Mexican Americans, began to arrive in Oregon towns and cities. This era marks the beginning of an economic contribution to the Willamette Valley by Latinos in the agricultural arena and to the present day in other areas of the local economy that have evolved through changing economic times. In the 1950sWoodburn felt the presence of Mexican Americans who were in search of jobs and opportunities. The majority of these Mexican Americans were farmworkers in search of work in fruitful agricultural ranches of Woodburn and its surrounding areas.

The interest in Oregon for these migrant farmworkers was the seasonal work they found along their migratory path of farm working. For some, Oregon became a stop along the way to Washington. Coming from California and the Southwest, these workers established a migratory cycle during the summers. By the 1960s few families came from Mexico; many of these traveling workers decided to settle in Woodburn, making this city their permanent home and investing in their future. However, in the past fifteen years that has no longer been the case. The population has grown to include families from Mexico and Central America. For these Mexicans and Central Americans, language is the common thread; they also share common experiences of work, religion, and food (Gamboa and Buan 1995).

Growth and Culture

As the town of Woodburn was beginning to see growth with the Latino population, certain services and organization started to appear in the community for these residents. The summer months were testament to this large population and St. Luke, the local Catholic Church, began to offer services in Spanish. Stores began to sell products used in Mexican cuisine, which was very important to these families. As the numbers increased, there was a natural need for cultural activities. By the early 1960s it was quite evident that these families would stay and enjoy all the town had to offer.

By now, according to Salinas, Woodburn Anglo merchants recognized the importance to foster new intercultural relationships. As the farmers increased their business the merchants also saw great profits from the Latino community. Thus Latinos could find a job for at least a few months out of the year, and so a new cycle began. As new relationships were constructed, the Woodburn merchants organized and promoted the first fiesta in honor of these new friendships. One may ask what the motives were for this fiesta and why the Anglo community hosted such an event. It was a simple gesture by a host community welcoming newcomers to Woodburn. Perhaps this new ethnic group was a novelty for Woodburn, and its members simply wanted to form basic human relationships. It was also to honor the Latino/Tejano community and an attempt at reciprocity between these two cultures. While the Anglo hosts had limited knowledge of the Latino culture, combined efforts were made so that the planning of the fiesta had familiar elements for the targeted audience. Eventually, the fiesta grew into a three-day tradition that lasted nearly forty years. The overall ambiance of Woodburn's Fiesta Mexicana is like the *fiestas del pueblo*, the festivals of small towns in Mexico and other Latin American countries. The components of a typical *fiesta del pueblo* incorporate elements of food, culture, folklore, entertainment—activities that reflect a familial environment. The fiesta in Woodburn allows people to feel a sense of belonging, capturing a sense of where they come and sharing it with non-Latinos.

Under the leadership of Russell W. Baglien the first committee was composed of Bud Stalnaker, Mary García, Reymundo Gómez, and Reymundo Gómez Jr. This gesture of gratitude on behalf of the local merchants has become the largest event in the area of Woodburn since 1964. The concept of the fiesta was initially intended to culminate understanding and appreciation between the Anglo and Latino communities (Salinas 2002).

In 1965, attendance at the fiesta was expected to grow, and it did. Tejano community members took a keen interest in leadership roles in the fiesta celebration, and by 1966 there was an official committee named the Latin American Club that organized the event. The founders of this committee were Concepción Olvera, Manuel Salazar, Léon Saldaña, and Andrea Schooler. This club is a nonprofit organization registered with the Chamber of Commerce in Woodburn. A Latin American Club in Portland offered informal technical assistance to the club in Woodburn. The mission of the fiesta was to improve education and employment, promote cultural events, improve the quality of life, and work as a nonprofit organization.

Through the decades some fiesta activities have changed and some have remained the same. Continuing elements include the parade on Saturday in downtown Woodburn, the presentation of the queen and her court, the food vendors, the entertainment, and the dances. However, a sign of change, which reflects local interests and cultural pastimes, is in the soccer match and the type of music heard throughout the days of the fiesta.

When the fiesta was initiated, Salinas recalls, and had a Tejano flavor, there was no soccer, and the music was popular with the Tejano culture—the sound of Tex Mex. Manuel Peña, an ethnomusicologist and professor of anthropology, describes Tex Mex music from a musical perspective and as a social process. Musically speaking,

> *Música tejana* is not one single music but several musical and musico-literary genres, ensembles, and their styles. It also includes two major regional ensembles—the *conjunto*, a close cousin of *música norteña*, and the Texas-Mexican version of the *orquesta*, a multi-styled wind ensemble patterned after the American swing band. (Peña 1999, xi)

Peña further explains that Tex Mex, like other styles of *música tejana*, is characterized by a homegrown quality, "and they all speak after their own fashion to fundamental social processing shaping Texas-Mexican society" (Peña 1999, xi).

The fiesta had baseball tournaments, a 5K race, freestyle wrestling (or *lucha libre*), and the Tex Mex sound that related to many working-class Tejanos. According to Salinas, the new immigrants could not relate to the same cultural activities that the Tejano pioneers of the first fiesta committee had established. During the 1970s, there was a notable change in composition of the Latino members of Woodburn. The Tejano pioneers witnessed an influx of Mexican immigrants arriving in Woodburn. As the Tejanos became a minority, the voice and face of the fiesta changed. The Mexican immigrants brought with them their cultural influences and interest reflected in banda music, the mariachi sound, and the favorite pastime of Latin America—soccer, introduced in the mid-1970s. While over the years there have been minor changes of these components the constant has remained to provide a family atmosphere for the event. Even more evidence of this grassroots community event is the fact that the fiesta has never been about large sponsorships or making profit. The Latin American Club committee members strive to maintain humble yet continuing efforts to keep the fiesta alive as a community tradition, one that all townspeople can be proud of.

Fiesta grew from curiosity and from trying to accommodate a new group in the valley. Changes also occurred in the leadership of the event. By the early 1970s the Latin American Club's leadership fell into the hands of the Latinos in the community yet remained some Anglo committee members (Miley 2002). With this new leadership the event also changed in composition and more Latinos started to attend the event. As mentioned before, the Latino pioneers of Woodburn were from Texas. As the decade of the 1980s began, the town of Woodburn started receiving immigrants from Mexico and a few from Latin America; this also transformed the elements of the fiesta. Before the late 1950s and early 1960s the music was the sound of Tex Mex. With the new influx of residents from Mexico mariachi music took over and eventually banda music followed. In the mid-1990s there was politically motivated dialogue concerning the growth of the event and the question was posed if the event should continue. Thus begins a shift in sentiment and intent reflecting the growth of Latinos in Woodburn. Thirty years earlier this cultural event began in the spirit of goodwill toward Latinos yet the political mind-set takes a turn in the face of growth.

However, in the mid-1990s, after an attendance growth, concerns about logistics of the fiesta are beginning to form and whether or not the fiesta can continue to be held in the present location. More and more one can see that because of population growth in this town issues of numbers reflect the challenges of parking, physical space capability, security, safety, and concerns of noise levels of nearby residents. According to Salinas, it is up to the Latin American Club leadership in conjunction with the Anglo community leaders to find alternatives and solutions to the current fiesta challenges due to the growth. The fiesta has always maintained and continues to firmly advocate for this event to be one that brings the Latino community together, a time for family, a time to socialize with friends and neighbors, to celebrate a heritage pride and for recent immigrants to feel and remember a slice of their county here in *el norte.*

One of the questions I posed was if this event is seen as an opportunity to have a cultural exchange with non-Anglos; the educational aspect of the fiesta was originally thought of as an important quality of the fiesta. To my surprise it is not. This event has become an exclusively Mexican and Mexican American event which did not begin as such. Perhaps it is in the first five years of this fiesta that there was a good mixture seen in the attendants of the celebration; people, including business merchants, from the surrounding areas like St. Paul and Gervais attended. The component of the businesspeople, the civic entities, the chamber of commerce, the education agencies are not visible as participants of the events or as supporters to the Latin American Club committee. In the past ten years, Woodburn, like other areas in Oregon, has experienced an explosion of Latino growth. There are roughly about 18,000 residents in Woodburn, half of whom are Latinos (Loy et al. 2001, 213). However, in the realm of the intellectual, financial, labor, and educational structures there has been little accommodation for this new growth. What has occurred is an influx of immigrants attracted by agricultural jobs, thereby changing the demographics and the face of a once Anglo-majority town. One of the challenges for the Tejano pioneers of this community is to preserve their roots and to educate newly arrived immigrants of their contributions to this town and the fiesta. Those who founded the Latino community in Woodburn of the 1950s and 1960s strive to educate the newly arrived Mexicans about the Tejano pioneers and the history of the presence of Latinos in Woodburn and the surrounding communities.

Extension of Identity and Community

Fiesta was not born of an interest to preserve the identity of the Latino community. This three-day event was created due to the interest from Anglo businesspeople to accommodate the new residents of the town. One can also suppose preserving the Tejano heritage was not on the minds of the migrants of the 1950s and 1960s. The Tejano pioneers came for survival purposes; they stayed for better opportunities. Along the way their roots were solidified in this town, new generations sprouted, and progressively the townspeople transplanted their ethnic identity onto the community and the Fiesta Mexicana. Today, there is no room to entertain whether the Mexican or Mexican American identity needs to be reinforced, it simply just is. In fact, Woodburn has been described by the local politicians as "little Mexico"; that alone says it all. This term is applied to many towns and cities across the United States to describe the Latino presence where these residents have captured and transferred a piece of their country of origin. The elements of everyday life like the twenty-four-hour Spanish language radio station, cable television that brings Spanish language programming, the grocery stores which carry household goods that one would find in Mexico, and agencies that provide services in Spanish—these are all facts that resonate identity and a strong Latino presence. Basically the media has made it possible to enhance a prevalent Mexican atmosphere in a small town like Woodburn. An ethnic identity for these Woodburn residents is a daily consumption; essentially Mexicanness is at everyone's fingertips. However, the enthusiasm to integrate and partake in a cultural event like the fiesta by non-Latinos is hardly felt. Since the early 1970s, when the fiesta experienced a shift in leadership, the participation of the Anglo community in Woodburn has been marginal. The lack of connection between the Anglos and the Mexican community has been a result of natural evolution. Throughout the years, beginning during the 1950s, there has been a strong and steady evolution of Tejano, Mexican American, and more recently a Mexican presence. The physical and cultural residence of this ethnic group implies that it brings with them a Spanish language, folklore, a value system, and a workforce, among many other things. Therefore, the center stage is being occupied by this ethnic group and less by the ancestors of the founding father George Settlemier. The disconnection is one that is bound to happen in a very natural and progressive manner unless opportunities like the fiesta are utilized by all to create cultural dialogue and understanding. The business and civic entities or education groups could promote and even sponsor the event. After all, the Mexicans and Mexican Americans represent a vital aspect of Woodburn and part of the labor force that is a vein of gold, critical to the economy of Woodburn. The ideal situation would be to have the Anglo community attempt at partaking in the fiesta but more extensively to be involved in the cultural exchange. Fomenting a positive relationship between Mexicans and Anglos in the Woodburn community would lessen misunderstandings and misconceptions from one group to another.

Overall, the target group of the fiesta is undeniably the Mexican and Mexican American population. This is a community that was launched into the fiesta as an entity that was to be accommodated but then the festival took a new life of its own with the direction of its own Mexican people and with the assistance of the Anglo community members. The significance of studying the fiesta as a cultural event for this community is one of cultural reunification. I would propose it is a fiesta that testifies to the mergence of a strong Mexican presence and the preservation of a historical Tejano presence. Moreover, it is an event that has grown to see the migratory influx of Latin Americans, Mexicans being the larger group. As with many cultural events one can only hope that the non-Latinos of this community are a collaborative catalyst for such a cultural exchange. For the Latinos of Woodburn the event assures a long-standing tradition that attests to an ever growing Latino population in western Oregon.

References

Dávila, Arlene M. 2001. *Latinos Inc.: The Marketing and Making of a People.* Berkeley, CA: University of California Press.

El Hispanic News y Más. 2002. Special Edition Program, August 2–4.

Gamboa, Erasmo, and Carolyn M. Buan. 1995. *Nosotros: The Hispanic People of Oregon Essays and Recollections.* Portland, OR: Oregon Council for the Humanities.

Loy, William G., Stuart Allan, Aileen R. Buckley, and James E. Meacham. 2001. *Atlas of Oregon.* 2nd ed. Eugene, OR: University of Oregon Press.

Miley, Bob. 2002. Interview by author. Woodburn, OR, September 10.

Miley, Cleo. 2002. Interview by author. Woodburn, OR, September 10.

Peña, Manuel. *Música Tejana.* 1999. College Station, TX: Texas A&M University Press.

Population Research Center, Portland State University. www.upa.pdx.edu/CPRC.

Salinas, Miguel. 2002. Interview by author. West Linn, OR, September 9.

Stoeltje, Beverly. 1992. *Folklore, Cultural Performances, and Popular Entertainments.* New York: Oxford University Press.

Te, Michelle. 2002."The Pioneer Spirit." *Woodburn Independent,* May 21.

U.S. Census Bureau. 2000. www.census.gov/main/www/cen2000.html.

10

Liberation Theology and Social Change: Chicanas and Chicanos in the Catholic Church

Gilbert R. Cadena and Lara Medina

Solidaridad es torrente que da vida / es mil Pueblos unidos al andar. Solidaridad es camino de esperanza / es proyecto de nueva sociedad.[1]

A HISTORY OF CONFLICT, RESISTANCE, AND ADAPTATION characterizes the relationship between Chicanas and Chicanos and the Roman Catholic Church.[2] As part of the largest ethnic group in the Catholic Church, Latinos and Chicanos make up the majority of Catholics in the southwestern United States. Today, however, Latinos are leaving the Church; they are joining evangelical and Pentecostal denominations, (re)turning to indigenous and African-based religions, or creating autonomous spiritual communities outside of organized religions. Those remaining are struggling to carve space for their identity and theology within the Church.

This chapter provides an introduction to some of the social changes and consequently theological changes taking place in the Catholic Church beginning in the 1970s through the lens of liberation theology. We then explore more recent factors causing the diminishment of liberation theology, yet the ongoing commitment to justice and a preferential option for the poor espoused by U.S. Latina/Latino theologians. The social forces influencing the relationship between social change and theology include the lasting impact of Latin American liberation theology, a small but growing critical mass of U.S. Latina/Latino theologians, and rapid demographic changes. When we first wrote this article in the early 1990s it appeared that a gradual institutional transformation was occurring, one characterized by social and religious conflict over the means of religious production. In other words,

Chicano and Chicana religious leaders were articulating a religious worldview challenging the status quo and power of the Euro American Catholic Church. While this is still the case, we have witnessed a backlash or return to conservative politics in the hierarchy of the Church that makes the work of Latina/Latino liberation theologians and pastoral workers extremely difficult.

To examine how this regression has occurred, we discuss the changing demographics of Catholics, theories of religion and social change, and liberation theology, and focus on a base community as an example of organizing in the socioreligious sphere.

Demographic Overview of Chicanas and Chicanos in the Catholic Church

Today, more than 70 percent of Chicanos identify as Catholic. Studies show that first-generation Mexicans have higher rates of Catholic affiliation when compared to second and subsequent generations of Chicanos. For example, in the National Latino Political Survey, 73 percent of Chicanos and 82 percent of Mexican born identify as Catholic. Protestants account for 16 percent of Chicanos and 8 percent of Mexicans (De la Garza et al. 1992). Both Chicanos and Mexicans receive significant guidance (62 percent) from religion, with only 6 percent of both groups stating they receive no guidance from religion (De la Garza et al. 1992).

Within the Catholic Church, Chicanos and Latinos composed about 40 percent of the Catholic Church (USCCB 2002). In the early part of the twenty-first century, Latinos will be about one-half of the Catholic laity. Over 71 percent of Catholic growth since 1960 is due to Latinos (NCCB 1999). More than a dozen (arch)dioceses are over 51 percent Latino and over twenty-seven (arch)dioceses are between 25 and 50 percent (NCCB/USCC 1990). According to the secretariat of Hispanic Affairs in Washington, DC, the following (arch)dioceses total over 50 percent Latino: Amarillo, Brownsville, Brooklyn, El Paso, Los Angeles, Las Cruces, Lubbock, Miami, Santa Fe, San Angelo, San Antonio, Tucson, and Yakima. Los Angeles represents the largest archdiocese in the United States, where Latinos total approximately 70 percent of the Catholic laity.

While the majority of Chicanos identified as Catholic from the mid-1800s, the hierarchy and religious leadership never reflected this relationship. The number of Chicana/Chicano priests, bishops, and sisters never developed into a critical mass. For example, about 3.8 percent of Catholic priests are Latino or about 1,818 out of 47,582 U.S. priests (USCCB 2002). Of these about 500 are U.S.-born Latinos. There is one Latino priest for every 9,925 Latino Catholics, compared to one Catholic priest for every 1,230 Catholics. Of

75,000 sisters, less than 750 are Latinas. Of the nearly 280 Catholic bishops about 9 percent, or twenty-five, are Latino. Of these, less than a quarter are Chicanos. From 1848 to 1970, the hierarchy appointed no Latino bishops, until Fr. Patricio Flores became auxiliary bishop in the San Antonio archdiocese. The ratio of Latino bishops to Latino Catholics is 1 million to one, compared to the general Catholic population where the ratio of bishops to parishioners is 231,000 to one. If we look at the pipeline of future Chicano priests and sisters and the pool of potential bishops, the numbers are not promising. While half of the dioceses claim to offer special programs in "Hispanic" ministry, Latinos only make up 11 percent of seminarians (NCCB 1999).

The Church today faces a significant loss of its clergy. From 1965 to 2005, the Church will lose 40 percent of ordained ministers, and the average age for ministers will be fifty-five (Schoenherr and Young 1993). At the same time, the Catholic Church will grow about 1 percent a year, due primarily to Latina fertility rates and immigration. Euro American Catholics will decrease in numbers, due to low fertility rates and an aging population. When comparing other ethnic Catholics, religious leadership remains concentrated among Irish Catholics. Irish Americans, for example, make up about 17 percent of the Church but total 49 percent of the bishops, 39 percent of the diocesan, and 34 percent of religious priests. German and Scandinavian Americans are about 20 percent of the Church, and total 25 percent of the bishops, diocesan, and religious priests (Greeley 1972).

Studies show that Catholics have achieved social and economic parity with Euro American Protestants. However, when income is controlled for ethnicity, differences vary among ethnic groups. For example, data from the General Social Survey show Italian, Irish, and Polish Catholic families earned more than Presbyterians, Episcopalians, Lutherans, Methodists, and Baptists. Only Jewish Americans earned more than Catholics. However, out of these groups, Latino Catholics earned the least with 57 percent of Italian Catholics (Greeley 1989).

Other studies show a general level of dissatisfaction and alienation from official Church activities. For example, mass attendance in most surveys shows a bimodal relationship in attendance. Among Chicanos, 41 percent attend mass at least once a month, and 47 percent never attend religious services. Mexican-born individuals have slightly higher attendance rates, with 51 percent attending at least once a month and 41 percent never attending mass. Gonzales and La Velle's national study found the vast majority (88 percent) of Latino Catholics not actively involved in parish activities and most (60 percent) not encouraged to be involved. Marin and Gamba found in San Francisco only 12 percent were very active in Church activities and over half (53 percent) dissatisfied with the priest in their current parish (1990).

Cadena's research on Chicano priests found a majority (58 percent) not satisfied with the way the Catholic Church responded to social problems in their community. Eighty-four percent of Chicano clergy feel Chicanos do not have an adequate voice in the decision-making process of the U.S. Catholic Church, and over 82 percent believe Chicanos are discriminated against by the Church (Cadena 1989). Throughout six generations, Gonzales and La Velle found 82 percent of Latino Catholics feel the Catholic Church should make greater efforts to include Latino culture and tradition in Church activities (1985).

The U.S. Catholic Church has attempted to minister and respond to Latino laity through the creation of diocesan Offices of Hispanic Affairs. Fifty-two percent of dioceses have such an office. Yet, closer examination reveals a less than serious effort by the Church. For example, in a study conducted by the secretariat for Hispanic affairs, most of these offices are located within another department, such as Catholic Charities. Almost 50 percent of the dioceses have no budget for Latino pastoral ministry. The number of priests, sisters, and pastoral workers working in Hispanic ministry is less than 1 percent of its diocesan personnel (NCCB/UCSC 1990).

An example of lack of control in the decision-making process is the unilateral elimination of the Los Angeles Archdiocese Office of Hispanic Ministry in 2002. While more than 70 percent of the archdiocese is Latino, the office was eliminated by Cardinal Roger M. Mahony due to a $5.7 million budget shortfall. There was no consultation with Latino staff, lay leaders, or clergy to respond to the cuts or develop alternatives. Rather than strengthen Latino ministry and leadership throughout the archdiocese, the Church has used the notion of "multiculturalism" as a way to diminish the growth of Latino influence.

The data reflect a Church stratified by ethnicity, class, and gender. An unequal distribution of power and the ethnic hegemony of the bishops and priests accounts for the near monopoly of the decision-making process in the Church. From seminaries to chancery offices, religious orders, and religious organizations, with few exceptions, Latinos remain segmented at each level. Yet, in spite of this stratification, many are creating avenues for social change by adhering to a Latina/Latino liberation theology. These liberationists, or advocates of liberation theology, participate in the process of transforming religious discourse by addressing inequalities affecting Latinas/os inside and outside of the Church.

Religion as a Source of Social Change

To understand how religion can be a source of social change, the writings of Italian social theorist Antonio Gramsci, Venezuelan sociologist Otto Maduro, and Cuban American theologian Ada María Isasi-Díaz are important to consider. For each of them, religion can serve as a catalyst in bringing about social change, as religious leaders join the side of subordinate groups and participate in socioreligious movements.

From Antonio Gramsci, the concept of hegemony helps explain the power and control of the Catholic Church. Hegemony refers to control over a group of people, not by forced domination but by consent through political and ideological leadership (Gramsci 1971). The laity internalizes the ideology of the hierarchy and believes their worldview is "natural" and legitimate. Church hegemony is reinforced in society with churches supporting the status quo of the state. The Church maintains its hegemony by controlling its religious leadership and through institutional discrimination. On the other hand, counterhegemony attempts to challenge the dominant worldview and contribute to ideological and structural change by a subordinate group. Liberation theology provides an example of counterhegemony by Latinos struggling against ethnic, gender, and class inequalities.

For Maduro, the "relative autonomy of religion" describes the dynamic relationship between religious institutions to society at large (1982, 87). All religious institutions are partially influenced by the dominant social forces of society; however, institutions remain partially independent of those forces. Sometimes this autonomous relationship seeks to create a more traditional worldview. For example, in 1967 Pope Paul VI reaffirmed the Church ban on contraception, despite the recommendation of a commission he appointed to study the reality of modern Catholic lives. At other times the autonomous relationship challenges the status quo and advocates a new religious or social system (e.g., Latin American liberation theology) that demands a "'preferential option for the poor" and a "political faith" to be lived by Christians.

Ada María Isasi-Díaz emphasizes the role of the community as the "real theologians" (Isasi-Díaz and Tarango 1988, 109). As actors and producers of religious thought, community members analyze the causes of oppression and link their religious understandings to social action. The "'theological technicians," or those trained in the academy, assist in this process. As enablers, they must be members of the community and remain accountable to the liberation of the community. This vision of leadership creates a radical shift in the use of power and the relationship of leaders to a community. Religious authority lies among the community, where social analysis and religious ideas are generated and clarified.

Liberation Theology

The production of U.S. Latino/Latina theology over the past three decades represents an example of religious cultural resistance and transformation where theologians, clerics, and laity use their social experiences as the starting point for theological discourse. For Latino/Latina liberationist theologians, traditional Euro American theology has failed to understand the culture and religiosity of U.S. Latinas/Latinos. It remains inadequate in addressing issues of class, racial/ethnic, gender, and religious inequalities. Liberation theology offers an alternative faith praxis for those estranged or alienated from the Roman Catholic Church.

Latin American liberation theology has significantly influenced the foundations of U.S. Latino/Latina theology. For Latin American theologians and advocates, the primary task of liberation theology is to free the oppressed from their inhumane living conditions. Generally, liberation theology seeks to (1) interpret the Christian faith from the perspective of the poor, (2) critique societal structures that cause poverty, and (3) critique the activity of the Church and of Christians through the lens of the poor (Berryman 1987). The motivating factors are compassion for the poor and "energetic" protest against the causes of collective oppression and the denial of basic human rights that are contrary to the plan of creation. Liberation theology calls for an authentic commitment to the struggle of the oppressed (Boff and Boff 1987). According to Gustavo Gutierrez, the first theologian to systematically write about liberation theology in 1971, liberation has three dimensions:

1. Liberation means freedom from oppressive economic, social, and political conditions.
2. Liberation means human beings take control over their own historical destiny.
3. Liberation includes emancipation from social sin and the acceptance of a life following Jesus' commitment to the poor. (Gutierrez 1973, 36–37)

There are two basic acts of this theology. The first act takes liberating action; the second reflects on the action in light of faith. Liberating action goes beyond charity or reform measures. The strategy of liberating action means the poor, subordinate groups, and those in solidarity with them, come together to understand the causes of their oppression and to organize themselves into groups or movements that challenge the unequal structures of society. The second act, faith reflecting on action, requires participants to question the role of Christianity in the strategies for liberation. In this act, faith seeks guidance through the Word of God as found in the Scriptures. Scriptures are read from the perspective of the poor and require a "theological-political rereading" of the Bible (Boff and Boff 1987, 33–34).

The doing of liberation theology can be further divided into three basic stages: (1) the socioanalytical stage, (2) the hermeneutical stage, and (3) the praxis stage. The socioanalytical stage requires an analysis of the actual conditions of poverty using the tools of Marxism to understand class struggle, economic factors, and the power of ideologies. The hermeneutical stage requires a reflection on what the Word of God has to say about the situation of oppression. Liberationists refer to the Scriptures by seeking the practical meaning of its contents for the purpose of application to contemporary social situations. The practical stage requires arrival at a specific course of action to be taken to rectify the oppressive situation. Action is essential to liberation theology as it sees the only true form of faith to be "political love" (Boff and Boff 1987, 39). In essence, this theology moves from the analysis of the social reality to seeking inspiration for action from the Bible to arriving at concrete strategies for action.

Contributions of U.S. Latina/Latino Theologians

Liberation theology began to have influence in the United States in the late 1960s and early 1970s. This coincided with the rise of the militant Chicano movement. However, as Chicano priests and Chicana sisters were being influenced by liberation theology, most Chicano activists and organizations severed ties to the Catholic Church. As an exception, César Chávez used his own piety, the power of Catholic symbolism, and the strength of the farmworkers' religious identity as a tool to fight the power of agribusiness.

It is important to understand the differences between Latin American liberation theology and U.S. Latino/Latina theology. First, the social context is different. Latin American liberation theology emerged from a context of extreme poverty and political turmoil in countries such as Brazil, Peru, Chile, Mexico, Nicaragua, and El Salvador. The liberating strategies required a focus on class oppression, the role of foreign multinational corporations, U.S. foreign policy, and Latin American oligarchies and military dictatorships. In the United States, the first writings by Chicano theologians in the late 1970s and early 1980s emphasized cultural survival within a historical legacy of racism (Elizondo 1983; Guerrero 1987). As Chicanas and Latinas began to write in the late 1980s and early 1990s, their experiences in confronting patriarchy and sexism as well as racism and classism influenced their theological contributions.

Liberation theology in both Latin America and the United States is concerned with social justice and the means to achieve it. However, in the United States the social and material conditions are not as extreme as in Latin America. In the United States Latino political movements tend to be reformist in nature, rather than revolutionary. Similarly, U.S. Latina/Latino liberationists give attention to group empowerment and social transformation rather than revolutionary change. A marked distinction is that the several Latino/Latina theologians in the United States have chosen not to name their theological works as liberation theologies, but simply U.S. Latino/Latina theology or Latina feminist theology. The tenets of liberation theology, however, remain central to their theological writings.

Virgilio Elizondo, a Chicano priest and the first theologian to write about Chicano socioreligious issues, suggests the source of creativity of the Chicano people lies in their *mestizaje*. As mestizos, Chicanos/Chicanas live on the outskirts of U.S. society. It is precisely the experience of being marginalized that calls Chicanas/Chicanos to challenge modern-day structures of oppression, including the Church (Elizondo 1983). Elizondo sees this as their prophetic call and mission:

> In fidelity to his [her] way, Mexican-American Christians are challenging the oppressive powers of today, both within the Latin American world and in the U.S.A. They do not want to inflict violence on others, but they know they have the mission to make known in no uncertain terms the injustice and violence that the establishments are inflicting. (Elizondo 1983, 104)

Elizondo's work highlights the role of mestizas/mestizos in creating a new reality, one that brings together the best of diverse cultures that make up the Chicano: the Indian, the Spaniard, the African, and the Asian. The mestiza/mestizo is one who bridges the gap between cultures and ethnic groups straddling two different cultures: the Mexican culture and the Euro American culture. Theologically speaking, he claims that Chicanos/as play a vital part in upholding the gospel, which brings about a reality of justice.

The contributions of Latina theologians have made a great impact on the course of U.S. Latina/Latino theology. In 1988, Ada María Isasi-Díaz and Yolanda Tarango wrote *Hispanic Women: Prophetic Voice in the Church.* The lives of Latinas and their religious understandings provide the foundation of this book. As feminists, these women seek to challenge patriarchal religious structures that exclude the experiences of women. Their contributions highlight the role of the Church in justifying patriarchy:

> The church sanctions—justifies—the patriarchy in society by being itself a patriarchal structure. If the church is holy and patriarchal, is not patriarchy holy? If the church were to denounce patriarchy, it would be an important moment in the process of the liberation of women. For this reason, as Roman Catholics we must continue to call the Catholic Church to repent of the sexism inherent in its structures and in some of its tenets. (Isasi-Díaz and Tarango 1988, x)

Their work articulates the religious motivations of Latinas and the praxis they engage in as they struggle toward liberation. This is a struggle not only to survive physically, economically, and culturally, but the struggle to be active agents in the making of their history. Religious understandings play an important role in Latina liberation as they provide the source of one's action in history. It is the sense of the divine in the lives of Latinas that gives them the strength for the struggle: "a struggle that is not a part of life but life itself" (Isasi-Díaz and Tarango 1988, 103).

As in liberation theology, praxis is critical to this theology. Action and reflection occur simultaneously during praxis. Accordingly, the emphasis is on "doing theology," which is to act in the world out of a commitment to the liberation of Latinas and oppressed communities. What represents justice for Latinas cannot be defined in conflict with what is justice for other communities of struggle. Community takes a primary role in this theology for several reasons. First, with experience as the starting point, it must include personal as well as communal experience. One without the other leads to individualism or abstraction. Second, liberation is linked to the full participation of humans in community, and third, community is an essential element of Latino culture, as it gives identity to Latinos in a hostile society (Isasi-Díaz and Tarango 1988).

The contributions made by Isasi-Díaz and Tarango represent the voices and experiences of women not traditionally included in theological discussions. Their work takes religious authority away from the exclusive realm of male academics and places it in the hands of Latinas whose faith and lived experiences inform their actions. The experiences of Latinas as the starting point radically challenge religious and academic structures to include these experiences in the norm of religious discourse.

Since the writing of this book, Isasi-Díaz uses the term "*mujerista* theology" to refer to her contribution to Latina theology. The name was chosen because *mujer* is most often used in the music of Latino cultures to refer to Latinas, whether it be protest songs or love songs. A *mujerista* makes a preferential option for women and struggles to liberate herself and other women. She works for justice and understands her call to bring forth a new people with strong women and strong men. *Mujerista* theology gives voice to their religious understandings always using "a liberative lens, which requires placing oneself radically at the core of our own struggling *pueblo*" (Isasi-Díaz 1989, 411).

Mujerista theology concerns itself with the issue of power and calls for a reinventing of power. For *mujeristas,* power "is the ability to enable all persons to become the most they themselves can be" and always in relationship to the community. This kind of power seeks to create "political, economic, and social conditions needed for the self-realization of all persons" (Isasi-Díaz 1989, 416). Power must be a shared power rather than power over others. Shared power lies in direct contrast to the kind of power that exists within the majority of structures influenced by patriarchy. As patriarchy is the institutionalization of male dominance over women, such structures require having a hierarchy of individuals with power over those on the bottom levels of the institution. *Mujeristas* condemn such abuse of power and call for the issue of power to be at the heart of theological discourse (Isasi-Díaz 1989).

While the term "feminist" accurately describes the perspective and vision held by *mujerista* theology, its authors felt the need to distinguish this theology from the term "feminism" or "feminist theology," as the latter had been identified with the Euro American women's focus on gender as the main oppressive element for all women. *Mujerista* theologians seek to emphasize the interlocking oppressions of racism, classism, and sexism that affect the lives of Latinas. Their distinct concerns necessitated a distinct terminology and naming process.

Since the first publication of what is now called *mujerista* theology, other Latina theologians have published their works and claim the term "feminist" for their theological understandings. In the most recent collection of Latina theologies, *A Reader in Latina Feminist Theology: Religion and Justice,* edited by María Pilar Aquino, Daisy Machado, and Jeanette Rodriguez, the editors clearly identify themselves as feminists and seek to eradicate the myth that Latinas are not feminists (2002). As Pilar Aquino writes, "The reality, however, is that Latina/Chicana and Latin American feminisms have been denied visibility and influence in the dominant theoretical construction of both U.S. feminism and Latino/Latina culture" (2002, 135). This collection of critical essays demonstrates the vitality and diversity of Latina religious thought and action. The authors draw from the richness of Chicana feminist discourse beginning in the early 1970s. Many of the contributors recognize the rich theological resource found in creative literature that Latinas inherit from the legacy of Sor Juana Inez de la Cruz as the first woman theologian in the Americas (Gonzáles 2002). Whether focusing on the creative works of Latinas or their daily experiences of crossing racial, class, gendered, and ideological borders in the United States, Latina theologians are concerned with justice, with the empowerment of women and their communities. Latina theology, whether identified as feminist or *mujerista,* does not exist merely to make Latinas feel good. It is theology concerned with challenging structures of oppression, whether in the private or public sphere. While there are variations within the umbrella term "Latina theology," the common element is concern for making justice a reality in the everyday lives of Latinas and their communities.

Other important U.S. Latina/Latino theologians making further contributions to this discourse include Roberto Goizueta, Orlando Espín, Gloria Loya, Allan Figueroa Deck, Arturo Banuelos, Fernando Segovia, Miguel De La Torre, Edwin Aponte, Michelle González, Nancy Pineda-Madrid, and Nora Lozano. It is beyond the scope of this chapter to summarize their work; however, each is making valuable strides in the development of Latina/Latino theology.

Calpulli: A Model for Social Change

Pastoral practitioners and community activists Rosa Marta Zarate, a Chicana religious sister, and Patricio Guillen, a Chicano priest, deserve recognition as religious leaders having an impact on U.S. Latina/Latino theology. Zarate and Guillen represent the community "'doing theology" with their involvement in the formation of base communities in San Bernardino County in Southern California. Base communities are small groups of people formed around theological reflection and community organizing. Involved in critical social analysis they link action to religious faith. These groups are modeled after the *comunidades eclesiales de base* of Latin American liberation theology, which formed as a result of the absence of clergy in the rural areas of Latin American countries. Religious leaders may take a role in the formation of these communities, but the emphasis rests on the laity taking leadership in the work of these small Church communities. Reflection, action, and worship are central aspects of these groups.

Since the early 1970s, Sr. Zarate and Fr. Guillen organized base communities in San Diego, San Bernardino, Imperial Valley, and Riverside, California. In the 1990s, they and a team of laypeople successfully applied the tenets of liberation theology by creating a system of profit and nonprofit cooperatives employing residents from the local community. Their goal is to create economically self-sufficient organizations that operate based on the principles of shared profit, shared responsibility, and shared power. The inspiration for their efforts comes not only from liberation theology but also from knowledge about the economic systems of their Mesoamerican ancestors. The cooperative system, or *calpulli,* of native communities provides the framework for much of the educational, economic, and cultural work that Zarate and Guillen facilitate. Their organizational plan includes establishing centers of learning and work that are owned and operated by the community. The philosophy behind *calpulli* stresses that social economic change is possible with the collective efforts of a community rather than individual workers.

Since 1987, the nonprofit centers focus on vocational training, English as a second language, youth employment training, continuing education, and immigrant services. The profit centers include a travel agency, tax and legal counseling, a bookstore, a gardening and landscaping service, clothing manufacturing, and food service. Decision making in the cooperatives uses a consensus model and all workers own a share of the cooperative.

A strong characteristic of *calpulli* is the emphasis placed on the indigenous cultural history of mestizos. *Calpulli* takes seriously indigenous knowledge and values existing prior to the European invasion in the Americas. Sr. Zarate, Fr. Guillen, and the members of *calpulli* seek to recover this knowledge and pass it on to the broader community. In the early 1990s, they intensified their learning and commitment to indigenous knowledge in a number of ways. For example, they coordinated a series of workshops for the community on the Mesoamerican system of *calpulli*. Dr. Clodomiro Siller, a Mexican anthropologist, led the workshops and initiated a study of the codices, the ancient sacred and historical books of Mesoamerica. In addition, they studied the *Relational Letters of Hernan Cortes*, the works of Bartolomé de Las Casas, and other historical documents. From their studies, a team wrote an open letter to the pope regarding the Roman Catholic Church's proposed 1992 Quincentennial Celebration. A four-page document was sent to the Apostolic Pro Nuncio, the papal representative to the United States, and published in several magazines and newsletters. The letter called for the institutional Church to

> ask forgiveness of the Indigenous peoples of America for the sins, past and present, committed against them. We further recommend that acts of reparation be included as integral to the commemoration of the encounter of cultures. These acts of reparation should be reflected in acts of solidarity with the struggles of the Indigenous of America in their efforts to redress the injustices committed against them. (Centro 1991, 4)

Calpulli also participated in the Peace and Dignity Journey, a spiritual run beginning simultaneously in Alaska and Argentina. The runners met in Mexico City on October 12, 1992, to commemorate 500 years of resistance by the indigenous people of the continent. Calpulli helped coordinate a team of runners to run a 180-mile link from San Bernardino to Blyth, California, and participated in the event. In the organizing of this event, contact was made with sixteen local indigenous groups living in southern California. Every four years the Peace and Dignity Journey is organized. In 2004, indigenous communities will unite with the Kuna Nation in Panama.

Calpulli seeks to create solidarity networks with other organizations seeking self-autonomy and self-determination for the purpose of empowering the poor and working for social change. They have relationships with campesino groups, Native American communities, community-based organizations, social scientists, universities, and student groups. Overall, *calpulli* seeks to educate, develop, and accompany the community as it seeks to create alternative social systems that provide sustenance and dignity for all involved.

In addition to community organizing, Sr. Zarate is an accomplished composer and singer of music that reflects the religious and political motivations of

Latinos struggling for justice. Her music is informed not only by Christian gospel values of justice, but also by Mesoamerican religious understandings. For example, a recent song speaks of the indigenous female deity, Cihuacoatl or To-nantzin, who remains a source of strength for many Chicanas and Chicanos:

> Tonantzin, mi nina.
> Llorona de tantos siglos,
> las rosas en el cerro florecen ya,
> la lucha del pueblo sera
> canto de victoria . . .
>
> Madre Tonantzin el Indio
> sigue de pié, resistiendo;
> y en su pisada andariega
> nadie ha podido vencerlo.
> La milpa sigue creciendo,
> alimentando esperanza.
> Y el Indio escribe su historia,
> al Indio nadie lo entierra.[3]

Zarate's artistic work is an example of Latina theology being informed by the aspirations of *el pueblo.*

Conclusion

This chapter shows that the Catholic Church is not a monolithic institution always promoting cultural conservatism. For liberationists, the struggle for cultural resistance and social change is carried out in their attempts to create an alternative worldview and challenge the religious structures of domination through praxis. This conscious transformation is an inseparable part of political and economic change. The emergence of liberation theology, the new critical mass of Latina/Latino theologians, and Latino demographic shifts all contribute to a movement for social change within the Church.

The relationship between Catholic hegemony and Latino counter-hegemony is important in understanding religious domination and ethnic group subordination. The Church is an example of a hegemonic institution through its control and maintenance of a system of ethnic, gender, and class inequality. In order for liberation theology to impact the lives of the masses of Latino Catholics, religious leaders must be active participants in social and political struggles, providing the organic link to grassroots communities. The methodology of praxis, theological reflection, and social action grounds their work to the lives and social context of Chicanas/Chicanos and Latinas/Latinos today.

While most Catholic theologians work primarily within the institutional framework of the Roman Catholic Church, it is important to recognize the non-Christian sources of religious expressions vital to the self-determination of Chicanas and Chicanos. Critical readings of indigenous sources such as the *Popol Vuh* and the numerous codices that portray the values of indigenous communities must be included in theological reflections. *Calpulli* successfully does this in their ministry. Many Chicanos, as mestizo peoples, often find their motivations and behavior come more from the ethics of indigenous ancestors than they do from the Christian influence. For example, the values of community, respect for elders, and religious observances represent indigenous "ethics" existing long before the Christian presence in the Americas. In addition, important values such as the relationship to the land, the valued role of homosexuals, or the role of female priestesses can be learned from native knowledge.

The ways in which Chicano Catholics create avenues for change within the institutional Church reflect the ongoing importance of religion in their lives, regardless of the historical alienation felt within the Catholic Church. Base communities, such as *calpulli*, create an environment of renewed religious commitment addressing the local, regional, and international concerns of its members. Although similar base communities are not the dominant model of Church in the United States, *calpulli* does provide an alternative model that has the capacity to strengthen the religious affiliation of many Latinos disaffected from the institutional Catholic Church. This relationship is based on collective action rather than abstract faith.

This relative autonomy of religion contributes to an emerging U.S. Latino theology, which allows particular groups in the Church to advocate a progressive religious and political agenda. As Latinas and Latinos transform the Church, the impact the Church has in society will reflect the social and religious interests of the future majority of U.S. Catholics.

Notes

1. "Solidarity is the power that gives life; it is a thousand communities walking united. Solidarity is the road of hope, the project of a new society." Rosa Martha Zarate Macias. Lyrics from "Solidaridad," *Concierto a mi pueblo* (San Bernardino, CA, 1990), cassette tape. Translated by authors.

2. This chapter uses the term "Chicano" to refer to the Mexican-origin population living in the United States. "Latino" is used when data cited or collective examples include Mexican-origin, Puerto Rican-origin, Cuban-origin, and other Latin American-origin populations.

3. "Tonantzin, my godmother. Crying woman of many centuries, the roses on the hillside still blossom, the struggle of the people will be the song of victory . . . Indian Mother Tonantzin continues by foot, resisting; and in your roving footsteps no one has been able to conquer you. The corn continues to grow, nourishing hope. And the Indian writes her history, the Indian will never be buried!" Lyrics by Rosa Martha Zarate Macias. "Tonantzin, Madre Tierra," *Abya Yala* (San Bernardino, CA, 1992), cassette tape. Translated by authors.

References

Aquino, María Pilar, Daisy L. Machado, and Jeanette Rodriguez, eds. 2002. *A Reader in Latina Feminist Theology: Religion and Justice*. Austin, TX: University of Texas Press.

Berryman, Phillip. 1987. *Liberation Theology*. New York: Pantheon.

Boff, Leonardo, and Clodovis Boff. 1987. *Introducing Liberation Theology*. Maryknoll, NY: Orbis.

Cadena, Gilbert R. 1989. "Chicano Clergy and the Emergence of Liberation Theology." *Hispanic Journal of Behavioral Sciences* 11: 107–21.

Centro de Reflexion e Investigación Pastoral Teologica. 1991. "An Occasion for Reflection: The 500 Years." Letter to Apostolic Pro Nuncio to the United States, August 1.

De la Garza, Rodolfo O., Louis DeSipio, E. Chris Garcia, John Garcia, and Angelo Falcon, eds. 1992. *Latino Voices: Mexican, Puerto Rican, and Cuban Perspectives*. Boulder: Westview.

Elizondo, Virgilio. 1983. *Galilean Journey: The Mexican American Promise*. Maryknoll, NY: Orbis.

Gonzales, Roberto O., and Michael La Velle. 1985. *The Hispanic Catholic in the United States*. New York: Northeast Catholic Pastoral Center for Hispanics.

González, Michelle A. 2002. "Seeing Beauty within Torment: Sor Juana Inés De La Cruz and the Baroque in New Spain." In *A Reader in Latina Feminist Theology: Religion and Justice*, ed. María Pilar Aquino, Daisy L. Machado, and Jeanette Rodriguez, 3–22. Austin, TX: University of Texas.

Gramsci, Antonio. 1971. *Selections from Prison Notebooks*. New York: International.

Greeley, Andrew. 1972. *The Catholic Priest in the United States: Sociological Investigations*. Washington, DC: United States Catholic Office.

———. 1989. *Religious Change in America*. Cambridge: Harvard University Press.

Guerrero, Andres G. 1987. *A Chicano Theology*. Maryknoll, NY: Orbis.

Gutierrez, Gustavo. 1973. *A Theology of Liberation*. Maryknoll, NY: Orbis.

Isasi-Díaz, Ada María. 1989. "Mujerista: A Name of Our Own." In *Future of Liberation Theology: Essays in Honor of Gustavo Gutierrez*, ed. Marc H. Ellis and Otto Maduro, 410–19. Maryknoll, NY: Orbis.

Isasi-Díaz, Ada María, and Yolanda Tarango. 1988. *Hispanic Women: Prophetic Voice in the Church*. San Francisco: Harper & Row.

Maduro, Otto. 1982. *Religion and Social Conflict*. Maryknoll, NY: Orbis, 1982.

Marin, Gerardo, and Raymond J. Gamba. 1990. *Expectations and Experiences of Hispanic Catholics and Converts to Protestant Churches.* Technical Report no. 2. San Francisco: University of San Francisco.

NCCB. 1999. *Hispanic Ministry at the Turn of the New Millennium.* A Report of the Bishops Committee on Hispanic Affairs. Washington, DC: National Conference of Catholic Bishops.

NCCB/USCC Secretariat for Hispanic Affairs. 1990. *National Survey on Hispanic Ministry.* Washington, DC: NCCB/USCC Secretariat for Hispanic Affairs.

Schoenherr, Richard, and Lawrence A. Young. 1993. *Full Pews, Empty Altars.* Madison: University of Wisconsin Press.

USCCB. 2002. *Encuentro and Mission: A Renewed Pastoral Framework for Hispanic Ministry.* Washington, DC: United States Conference of Catholic Bishops.

Index

About the Contributors

Gilbert R. Cadena is professor of Ethnic and Women's Studies at California State Polytechnic University, Pomona. He is coeditor *of Old Masks, New Faces: Religion and Latino Identity* (Bildner Center for Western Hemisphere Studies, 1995). His research interests include liberation theology, religious leadership, Chicanos and the Catholic Church, and Días de los Muertos.

Roberto M. De Anda is assistant professor in the Chicano/Latino Studies Program at Portland State University. In addition to continuing his research on labor market inequality among Mexican-origin workers, he is currently engaged in a study of Ernesto Galarza, a noted Mexican scholar, labor organizer, community activist, and educator in the United States. De Anda is the author of several articles and book chapters on underemployed—jobless, involuntary part-time, and working poor—men and women of Mexican descent.

Janie Filoteo is a doctoral candidate in the Department of Sociology at Texas A&M University. Her research interests include race and ethnicity, demography, and gender. Her current research examines the portrayal of gender in mass media. Specifically, she is analyzing the intersection of race, class, and gender in magazine advertisements. Her dissertation will focus on women in the workforce.

Elizabeth Flores is assistant professor in the Department of Humanities at Grand Canyon University. Her research involves such areas as literary studies, cultural studies, and gender studies. Her work concentrates on the literary production and analysis of Chicana/Latina autobiographical narratives. Her most recent publication is an autobiographical narrative of her experience in higher education as a woman of color, "A View from the Ivory Tower: A Latina's Experience in Higher Education," forthcoming in *Ingrates at the Gates: People of Color in Higher Education Talk Back.*

Lara Medina is assistant professor of religious studies at California State University, Northridge. She is currently at work on *Las Hermanas: Chicana/Latina Religious-Political Activism.* Her earlier research and publications focus on Chicana spirituality and ritual, U.S. Latina/Latino theology, Chicano religious history, and Días de los Muertos.

Maria Cristina Morales is a doctoral student in the Department of Sociology at Texas A&M University. Her research areas of interest include immigration, labor, and social inequality. Her dissertation research focuses on the relationship between employment in coethnic workplaces and the labor market outcomes among Latino and Asian immigrants.

Robert P. Moreno is associate professor in the Department of Child and Family Studies at Syracuse University. His research examines familial and cultural influences on children's learning and academic achievement among Latinos and low-income families. His recent publications include coediting a special issue of the *Hispanic Journal of Behavioral Sciences* (May 2002) and a chapter titled "Chicano Families and Schools: Myths, Knowledge, and Future Directions for Understanding," in *Chicano School Failure and Success: Past, Present, and Future*, edited by R. Valencia.

Gilda Laura Ochoa is an assistant professor of sociology and Chicana/ Chicano Studies at Pomona College. She has published qualitative research on intraethnic relations between Mexican Americans and Mexican immigrants in *Social Science Quarterly and Frontiers: A Journal of Women Studies.* Her forthcoming book, tentatively titled *Becoming Neighbors: Power, Conflict, and Solidarity in a Mexican American Community*, focuses on the factors and situations influencing intraethnic relations.

Eric Romero is a doctoral candidate in the Department of Anthropology at the University of Arizona. He is presently working as an associate for the Center for the Education and Study of Diverse Populations at New Mexico Highlands University. His areas of research include rural Chicanos, place-based education, discourse and narrative analysis, and bilingualism in New Mexico.

Rogelio Saenz is professor and head of the Department of Sociology at Texas A&M University. His research interests include demography and social inequality. He is currently analyzing demographic changes in the Latino population. His recent work has appeared in *Great Plains Research, International Migration Review, Rural Sociology, School Psychology Quarterly, Southern Rural Sociology,* and *Social Science Quarterly.*

Armando L. Trujillo is associate professor in the Division of Bicultural-Bilingual Studies at the University of Texas at San Antonio. Trained as a sociocultural anthropologist, his research interests include community studies, ethnicity, anthropology of schooling, community-based organizations, and ethnographic research methods. He is the author of *Chicano Empowerment and Bilingual Education: Movimiento Politics in Crystal City, Texas.*

Elsa O. Valdez is a professor of sociology at California State University at San Bernardino. Her areas of specialization include the Chicano/Latino family, the sociology of education, and race and ethnic relations. A recent publication is "Winning the Battle, Losing the War: Bilingual Teachers and Post-Proposition 227" in *Urban Review.* She also has two other recent publications in *Perspectives in Mexican American Studies* and *VOCES: A Journal of Chicana/Latina Studies.*

Raúl Homero Villa is associate professor in the Department of English and Comparative Literary Studies at Occidental College in Los Angeles, California. His research and teaching interests are in contemporary Chicano literature, popular culture, and cultural studies. His book, *Barrio-Logos: Space and Place in Urban Chicano Literature and Culture,* was published in 2000.